TEACHERS AND TESTING

TEACHERS
AND
TESTING

by David A. Goslin
RUSSELL SAGE FOUNDATION

Russell
Sage
Foundation

NEW YORK 1967

Printed in the United States of America
by Connecticut Printers, Inc., Hartford, Conn.

Library of Congress Catalog Card Number: 67–25912

Contents

Acknowledgments   *xix*

1

INTRODUCTION   *1*

2

THE USES OF STANDARDIZED TESTS IN SCHOOLS   *12*
The extent of testing   13
The use made of the results   19
The reporting of test scores to pupils and parents   25
The reporting of test scores to teachers   32

3

EXPERIENCE OF TEACHERS WITH TESTS AND TESTING   *33*
Formal training in measurement techniques   34
Familiarity with tests   38
Experience in administering tests   42
Background in relation to teachers' familiarity and experience   46

4

THE OPINIONS OF TEACHERS ABOUT TESTS   *49*
The nature of tests and intelligence   50
Accuracy   50
Relevance of tested intelligence to qualities necessary for success in school and after school   54
Genetic vs. learning components in tested intelligence   59

v

Testing practices 60
The number of tests being given 61
The weight to be given test scores 63
The use of tests to evaluate teachers 70
The use of test scores in assigning grades 71
*Providing pupils and pupils' parents with intelligence
test scores* 72

5

THE ROLE OF TEACHER AS TEST USER   79
The use of test scores in grading 80
Advising students about course work 82
*Providing students and parents with information about
their abilities* 87
Access to intelligence test scores 88
*Providing pupils and their parents with intelligence
test information* 89
*Requests from pupils and their parents for test
scores* 96
*Pupil and parent knowledge of intelligence test
scores* 97
The card sort test 98
*Card sort scores vs. teacher reports of test score
use* 100
*Card sort scores vs. teacher opinions and background
characteristics* 102
*Card sort scores vs. school and testing program
characteristics* 105

6

THE TEACHER AS A COACH FOR TESTS   *107*
*Teacher opinions about their responsibility to prepare
pupils for standardized tests* 109
*Teacher reports of the extent to which they attempt
to prepare pupils for tests* 111
*Student reports of the extent to which teachers have
attempted to prepare them for tests* 119

Teacher reports of requests to prepare pupils for standardized tests 121
Teacher uses of objective vs. essay tests 122

7

CONCLUSION   **126**

Teacher training in measurement techniques and theory 127
Opinions concerning the nature of intelligence and accuracy of tests 129
Teacher uses of tests 133
Coaching for tests 137
Opinions vs. practices 138
Teachers, testing, and the school 139

APPENDICES   *141*

I   *Sampling and data collection procedures—secondary schools* 143
II   *Teachers' questionnaire* 153
III *Testing program questionnaire* 186
IV *Familiarity of secondary school teachers with various standardized ability, personality, and interest tests* 193

Index 197

Tables

Table 1: *Percentage of public secondary schools that report giving various types of standardized tests to pupils in grades 10, 11, and 12* 14

Table 2: *Percentage of public secondary schools that responded "yes" to the question, "Are standardized achievement tests given in grades 10, 11, and 12 in your school in one or more of the following fields?"* 15

Table 3: *Average number of hours spent by public secondary school pupils taking standardized tests during the twelfth-grade year according to school reports* 15

Table 4: *Percentage and number of various standardized tests given in 714 public elementary schools to preschool children and children in grades kindergarten to six, by type of test* 16

Table 5: *Reports of public secondary school administrators of the importance of various reasons for the use of standardized tests in their school* 20

Table 6: *Reports of public secondary school administrators of the frequency with which standardized test scores are used for various purposes in their school* 21

Table 7: *Percentage of time various uses are reported for each type of test in 714 public elementary schools* 22

Table 8: *Public secondary school policy on the extent to which standardized test scores are reported to pupils and parents* 26

Table 9: *Public secondary school counselor reports of school practices concerning the reporting of standardized test scores to parents, by type of test* 26

ix

Table 10: Grade vs. policy on reporting of test scores to parents in public elementary schools, by test — 28

Table 11: Grade vs. policy on reporting of test scores to children in public elementary schools, by test — 29

Table 12: Type of test vs. policy on reporting of test scores to parents, by test, for all grades in 714 public elementary schools — 30

Table 13: Type of test vs. policy on reporting of test scores to children, by test, for all grades in 714 public elementary schools — 31

Table 14: Responses of secondary school teachers, public secondary school counselors, and elementary school teachers to the question, "Approximately how many graduate or undergraduate courses in the following general area have you had: tests and measurements (sample course titles: individual testing, analysis of the individual, psychological measurements, diagnostic testing, group tests and techniques, mental measurements, personality testing, etc.)?" — 35

Table 15: Responses of secondary school teachers, public secondary school counselors, and elementary school teachers to the question, "Approximately how many graduate or undergraduate courses in the following general area have you had: methods of research (sample course titles: research in education, statistical methods in education and psychology, statistics, educational statistics, methods in educational research, research design, etc.)?" — 36

Table 16: Responses of secondary school teachers and elementary school teachers to the question, "Have you ever attended any clinics or meetings intended primarily to acquaint teachers with the content, philosophy, or methodology of standardized testing (not counting courses taken in college or graduate school)?" — 37

Table 17: Distribution of public, private, and parochial secondary school teachers on the index of familiarity with tests — 39

Table 18: Responses of secondary school teachers and public secondary school counselors to the questions, "Have you ever examined a complete copy of: A. The College Board Scholastic Aptitude Test (SAT)?" B. The National Merit Scholarship Qualifying Test?" C. Any of the tests in the American College Testing Program?"   40

Table 19: Responses of secondary school and elementary school teachers and public secondary school counselors to the question, "Have you ever taken the SAT?"   41

Table 20: Responses of secondary school teachers and public secondary school counselors to the question, "Have you ever seen a copy of the booklet, 'A Description of the College Board Scholastic Aptitude Test' (published by Educational Testing Service)?"   42

Table 21: Percentage of secondary school teachers and counselors and public elementary school teachers who report having personally administered various types of standardized tests since they began teaching or counseling   43

Table 22: Percentage of secondary school teachers and public secondary school counselors and elementary school teachers who are routinely responsible for administering various kinds of standardized tests   44

Table 23: Distribution of public, private, and parochial secondary school teachers on the index of experience in administering and scoring tests   46

Table 24: Comparison between familiarity of public secondary school teachers with tests and reported number of courses taken in tests and measurements   47

Table 25: Responses of secondary school teachers, public secondary school counselors, and elementary school teachers and principals to the question, "How accurate do you (personally) feel most standardized intelligence or aptitude tests are in measuring a student's potential?"   51

Table 26: Responses of secondary school teachers, public secondary school counselors, and elementary school teachers to the question, "Which one of the following kinds of information do you feel provides the SINGLE MOST ACCURATE measure of a student's intellectual ability?"   52

Table 27: *Responses of American adults, public, private, and pa-rochial secondary school students, and elementary school parents to the question, "What has been most important to you in deciding how intelligent you (or your children) are?"*   53

Table 28: *Responses of secondary school students, teachers, and counselors, and elementary school teachers and parents to the question, "How important do you feel the kind of intelligence measured by intelligence tests is for success in school or college?"*   56

Table 29A: *Responses of secondary school teachers and public secondary school counselors to the question, "How important do you feel the kind of intelligence measured by standardized tests is for success in one of the professions, such as law or medicine?"*   57

Table 29B: *Responses of secondary school teachers and public secondary school counselors to the question, "How important do you feel the kind of intelligence measured by standardized tests is for success in the business world?"*   57

Table 30: *Responses of American adults, secondary school students, teachers, and counselors, and elementary school teachers and parents to the question, "Do you think intelligence tests measure the intelligence a person is born with or what he has learned?"*   58

Table 31: *Responses of secondary and elementary school teachers to the question, "How do you feel about the number of school-sponsored standardized tests that are given in your school?"*   61

Table 32: *Responses of secondary and elementary school teachers to the question, "How do you feel about the amount of use that is made of scores on school-sponsored standardized tests in your school?"*   62

Table 33: *Opinions of public, private, and parochial secondary school teachers on the amount of weight to be given various pupil indicators for different purposes*   64

Table 34: *Percentage of public, private, and parochial secondary school teachers in each quartile of the distribution of scores on each of the various weight indices*   68

Table 35: Responses of secondary and elementary school teachers to the question, "How do you feel about the use of standardized achievement test scores by school administrators for evaluating the effectiveness of teachers?" 71

Table 36: Opinions of public secondary school teachers on the use of tests to evaluate teachers' effectiveness, by school policy concerning the use of achievement tests to evaluate teachers 72

Table 37: Responses of elementary school teachers to the questions, "Do you think that teachers should consider their pupils' intelligence test scores in assigning grades?" and "Do you think that teachers should consider their pupils' standardized achievement test scores in assigning grades in their courses?" 73

Table 38A: Opinions of secondary and elementary school teachers on whether teachers should give a student specific information about his intelligence 73

Table 38B: Opinions of secondary and elementary school teachers on whether teachers should give a student general information about his intelligence 74

Table 38C: Opinions of secondary and elementary school teachers on whether teachers should give a pupil's parents specific information about the pupil's intelligence 74

Table 38D: Opinions of secondary and elementary school teachers on whether teachers should give a pupil's parents general information about the pupil's intelligence 75

Table 39: Responses of secondary school teachers to the question, "Do you feel that teachers, counselors, psychologists, etc. should give high school students specific information concerning their intelligence?" 75

Table 40: Responses of secondary and elementary school teachers to the question, "Do you feel that teachers ought to have their pupils' IQ scores? 76

Table 41: Responses of secondary school students to the question, "Do you think that high school students should be given specific results of their performance on intelligence tests?" 77

Table 42: Responses of elementary school parents to the question, "Do you feel that parents should be given specific information concerning their children's performance on intelligence tests?" 78

Table 43: Responses of elementary and secondary school teachers to the question, "Have you ever considered a pupil's intelligence test score in assigning him a grade in one of your classes?" 80

Table 44: Responses of secondary school teachers to the question, "Have you ever considered a pupil's college-admissions test scores as one basis for assigning him a grade in one of your classes?" 80

Table 45: Responses of secondary and elementary school teachers to the question, "Have you ever made use of a pupil's intelligence test score in advising him about his work in your course?" 82

Table 46: Experience of public secondary school teachers in administering and scoring tests, by use of intelligence test scores in advising students about course work 84

Table 47: Familiarity of public secondary school teachers with tests, by use of intelligence test scores in advising students about course work 84

Table 48: Opinions of public secondary school teachers about accuracy of intelligence tests, by use of intelligence test scores in advising students about course work 85

Table 49: Opinions of public secondary school teachers on whether intelligence tests measure inborn intelligence or learned knowledge, by use of intelligence test scores in advising students about course work 85

Table 50: Responses of secondary and elementary school teachers to the question, "Have you ever known any of your pupils' intelligence test scores?" 88

Table 51: Responses of secondary and elementary school teachers to the question, "In general, do you feel that you have an accurate estimate of how intelligent your students are?" 89

Table 52: Responses of secondary and elementary school teachers to the questions, "Have you ever given a student specific information about his intelligence?" and "Have you ever given a pupil general information about his intelligence?" 90

Table 53: Responses of secondary and elementary school teachers to the questions, "Have you ever given a parent specific information about his child's intelligence?" and "Have you ever given a parent general information about his child's intelligence?" 91

Table 54: Practice of public secondary school teachers in giving students general information about their intelligence, by familiarity with tests 93

Table 55: Practice of public secondary school teachers in giving students general information about their intelligence, by experience in administering and scoring tests 93

Table 56: Practice of public secondary school teachers in giving students general information about their intelligence, by teacher opinions about giving students general information about their intelligence 94

Table 57A: Responses of secondary and elementary school teachers to the question, "How often do your pupils ask you for information about their abilities?" 96

Table 57B: Responses of secondary and elementary school teachers to the question, "How frequently do parents of your pupils ask you for information about their children's abilities?" 96

Table 58: Responses of secondary and elementary school teachers to the question, "Do you feel that your students have an accurate estimate of how intelligent they are?" 97

Table 59: Responses of secondary and elementary school teachers to the question, "Have you ever had a student indicate to you that he did not know how intelligent he was?" 98

Table 60: Distribution of scores of secondary school teachers on the card sort test 100

Table 61: Public secondary school teachers' use of intelligence test scores in advising pupils about work in a course, by card sort test score   101

Table 62: Public secondary school teachers' opinions about the accuracy of intelligence tests, by card sort test score   103

Table 63: Public secondary school teachers' opinions about whether the kind of intelligence necessary to do well on standardized intelligence tests is inborn or learned, by card sort test score   104

Table 64: Index of extent of test use by public secondary school teachers' card sort test score   105

Table 65: Index of extent of testing by public secondary school teachers' card sort test score   106

Table 66: Responses of secondary and elementary school teachers and public secondary school counselors to the question, "Do you feel that teachers have a responsibility to try to prepare their students specifically for standardized aptitude or intelligence tests?"   109

Table 67: Responses of secondary and elementary school teachers and public secondary school counselors to the question, "Do you feel that teachers have a responsibility to try to prepare their students specifically for standardized achievement tests?"   110

Table 68: Responses of secondary and elementary school teachers to the question, "If you were to discover that a standardized achievement test which is used for college admission differed in its emphasis on your field from the present content of your course in this subject, do you feel you would change your course in any way?"   110

Table 69: Opinions of public secondary school teachers of teachers' responsibility to prepare students specifically for standardized tests, by familiarity with tests   111

Table 70: Opinions of public secondary school teachers of teachers' responsibility to prepare students specifically for standardized tests, by opinion on the accuracy of intelligence or aptitude tests in measuring a student's potential   112

Table 71: Opinions of public secondary school teachers of teachers' responsibility to prepare students specifically for standardized tests, by total test weight   112

Table 72: Public, private, and parochial secondary school teachers who say "yes" to three questions about preparing pupils for standardized tests   113

Table 73: Responses of secondary and elementary school teachers to the question, "Has your knowledge of the content of one or more standardized achievement tests in your field ever caused you to alter the content of the courses taught by you?"   114

Table 74: Responses of secondary and elementary school teachers to the question, "Has your knowledge of the content of one or more standardized achievement tests in your field ever caused you to change your teaching methods (but not the content of your courses)?"   115

Tabel 75A: Public secondary school teachers' reports of having prepared students for standardized tests by teaching them how to take tests, by familiarity with tests   116

Table 75B: Public secondary school teachers' reports of having prepared students for standardized tests by teaching them how to take tests, by experience in administering and scoring tests   116

Table 76A: Public secondary school teachers' reports of having changed their teaching methods because of knowledge of the content of standardized achievement tests, by familiarity with tests   117

Table 76B: Public secondary school teachers' reports of having changed their teaching methods because of knowledge of the content of standardized achievement tests, by experience in administering and scoring tests   117

Table 77: Public secondary school teachers' reports of having prepared students for standardized tests by teaching them how to take tests, by index of extent of testing   118

Table 78: Public secondary school teachers' reports of having prepared standardized tests, by school policy on giving parents information on pupils' aptitudes for learning school subjects   118

Table 79: *Public secondary school teachers' reports of having prepared students for standardized tests, by school policy on importance of tests to section pupils in any given grades by level of mental ability*   119

Table 80: *Responses of public, private, and parochial secondary school teachers to the question, "Have you ever been asked by any of your pupils to alter the content of any of your courses so that they would be better prepared for standardized tests?"*   122

Table 81: *Responses of public, private, and parochial secondary school teachers and elementary school teachers to the question, "How frequently do you use objective (that is, multiple-choice, true-false, matching, or completion) questions in tests that you prepare for your students?"*   123

Table 82: *Responses of public, private, and parochial secondary school teachers, and elementary school teachers to the question, "How frequently do you use essay or short essay questions in tests that you prepare for your students?"*   124

Acknowledgments

THE RUSSELL SAGE FOUNDATION PROGRAM of research on the social consequences of testing, of which this study is a part, was jointly supported by Carnegie Corporation of New York and Russell Sage Foundation. In addition, support for the field work phase of the survey of secondary school students, teachers, and guidance counselors was provided by the Cooperative Research Branch of the United States Office of Education through a grant to the University of Pittsburgh and the American Institute for Research.

As in any large scale research endeavor, a great many people contributed in large measure to its outcome. The secondary school survey was carried out by the Project Talent field staff under the supervision of Isidore Goldberg and William W. Cooley. Dr. Goldberg, in particular, provided invaluable assistance in the construction of questionnaires and did an extraordinary job of obtaining the cooperation of schools and facilitating the process of data collection. In addition, I am indebted to John T. Dailey and John C. Flanagan of Project Talent and the American Institute for Research for their help in the initial stages of the project.

The overall program of research on the social effects of testing is under the direction of Orville G. Brim, Jr., president of Russell Sage Foundation. To him I once again owe a special debt of gratitude—for his continued support, enthusiasm, and assistance at every stage of the project. In addition, I am grateful to David C. Glass, Ira Firestone, Robert K. Merton, and Roger Lennon for the many hours they spent reading the manuscript and for their uniformly helpful suggestions and criticisms.

Roberta R. Epstein and Barbara A. Hallock played important roles in the elementary school phase of the research, and Robert Washington assisted in the analysis of survey data from both studies. I am indebted to Barbara Boone for her help in the statistical analysis of the data, and for her careful work on the first draft of the manuscript. The final product owes much to the energy and enthusiasm of my secretary, Eleanor Kuhn. Finally, I am especially grateful to Margaret Dunne, Russell Sage Foundation's incomparable editor, for making the task of final preparation and production so easy.

Although I take full responsibility for any shortcomings of the research and the report thereof, it could not have been done without the enthusiasm, guidance, and assistance of those I have mentioned. With respect to whatever contribution this report might make, it is their achievement as well as mine.

David A. Goslin
RUSSELL SAGE FOUNDATION

May 24, 1967

xix

1

Introduction

FROM THE earliest beginnings of society, men have measured the abilities of other men and have recognized the existence of differences in the abilities possessed by different individuals. As human societies have grown in size and complexity the recognition of individual differences has increasingly been reflected in the social structure of societies. Ability is not the only basis on which social differentiation occurs, of course, and it has only been in the past half-century in the most highly developed societies that attempts have been made systematically to evaluate intellectual abilities and to make use of this evaluation as a basis for allocating individuals to positions in the society.

As we have pointed out elsewhere,[1] all societies must train their members to perform the tasks necessary for the continuation and development of the society. In addition, they must provide for the allocation of individuals to positions in the society. The importance of these two functions is reflected in the fact that, to the best of our knowledge, no society leaves the development and allocation of manpower to chance, although a great variety of means have been, and are, used to accomplish these ends. In general, the techniques by which individuals are channeled into one position or another (and frequently given opportunities for one kind of training as opposed

[1] Goslin, David A., *The School in Contemporary Society*. Scott Foresman and Co., Chicago, 1965, pp. 106–107.

1

to another) may be classified into those that are based largely on ascribed (or inherent) characteristics of the individual and those that are based on his achievements or performance. In primitive societies, and to a lesser but still significant extent in our own society, an ascribed characteristic on which many important distinctions are made is sex, women immediately being eliminated as candidates for many positions in the society (the same holds true, of course, for men). Similarly, race, age, class, religion, birth order, and ethnic group membership all are likely to play a more or less important part in the process of status ascription in modern as well as primitive societies.

Since the adequate performance of most adult roles requires considerable training, particularly in technologically advanced societies, it may be postulated[2] that the earlier a person's training for a position begins, the more successful and complete it is likely to be, and consequently the more able he will be to perform his duties. Support for this proposition may be adduced from the fact that, historically, prospective allocation to positions in the society has more often than not preceded the acquisition of the requisite skills, as in the case of the apprenticeship system and, in advanced societies, selective admission to college. The intimate relationship between the development of well-trained manpower and the most efficacious allocation of that manpower is made more salient as the society becomes more technologically complex and both the skills necessary and the amount of training involved in the successful performance of many roles are multiplied.

In the United States concern with the measurement of abilities, and, in particular, intellectual skills, has grown steadily during the past forty or fifty years. At present, from the time a child enters school until he graduates from high school or college and enters the work force his intellectual abilities are constantly being evaluated and re-evaluated. In no other society do we find as great a preoccupation with accurate assessment of ability combined with the allocation of opportunity for advancement in the society on the basis of ability. We have not as yet reached the point where a person's chances for success are completely determined by his abilities.

[2] This point is taken from Linton's classic analysis of status and role in human society. See Linton, Ralph, *The Study of Man*, D. Appleton-Century Co., New York, 1936.

Ascribed characteristics such as family background, race, and sex still play an important part in the allocation process for many individuals, but we have gone farther in this direction than any other nation, with the possible exception of the Soviet Union.[3] And we have certainly done more about developing systematic techniques for assessing abilities than any other society.

The development of standardized tests of ability has been a major factor in this process in the United States. A person's abilities may be assessed by various means, the most obvious of which is his performance in the position for which he is a candidate. As we have pointed out, however, it is increasingly becoming impractical to give everyone a chance to try out for every position, especially as the training required for most jobs becomes more complex and expensive. The result is the necessity for devising some way to predict which individuals are best suited for which jobs before providing them with the required training. One alternative is to use performance in school as an indicator of general ability, and to allocate opportunities for further training, leading to high status positions in the society, on the basis of this performance. It has long been recognized, however, that teacher judgments of pupils are often subjective and based on characteristics unrelated to the abilities of the person being evaluated. In addition, standards vary from school to school and from teacher to teacher within schools. The solution to these problems has been the development of standardized, objective tests of ability which may be used to assess the capabilities of large numbers of students having varying educational backgrounds.

Standardized ability tests, including intelligence and achievement measures, have been almost universally adopted by educational systems in this country. It has been estimated that each of the fifty million or more school children in the United States takes,

---

[3] The case of the Soviet Union provides an interesting comparison with the United States. Although Russia, as a consequence of rapid industrialization, has moved in the direction of efforts to assess individual abilities, political ideology in the Soviet Union is incompatible with the notion of inherited differences in abilities between individuals. Consequently, assessment, where it occurs, has tended to focus on achievement differences, assumed to be based on differential motivation and individual effort rather than on innate variability. Taking the position that all variation in performance is due to differences in motivation permits one to concentrate most of one's effort on devising techniques for raising motivation levels while de-emphasizing systematic assessment, particularly at early ages. See Goslin, David A., *The Search for Ability: Standardized Testing in Social Perspective*, Russell Sage Foundation, 1963, chap. 2.

on the average, three standardized tests each year.[4] Testing practices differ widely from school district to school district and from
grade to grade with school systems. This means that some children
are exposed to more than three standardized tests in a given school
year while some take fewer or none. Nevertheless, it is a rare child
indeed whose abilities are not formally tested on several occasions
by the time he finishes secondary school.

Scores on standardized tests are used by schools and colleges
for admission purposes (not only to college, but to special elementary and secondary schools as well), for grouping children according to their abilities for instructional purposes, for counseling pupils
and parents, and for a variety of other purposes, including identifying pupils with special educational deficiencies and strengths.[5] It is
generally acknowledged that standardized tests in current use are
less than perfect instruments for evaluating a given individual's
capabilities. But there is strong evidence that in many instances
they are better than any alternative device available and, in most
cases, used in conjunction with pupil grades, they increase the likelihood of making accurate predictions of a pupil's future academic
performance.[6]

Given the extent of test use and the importance of the kinds
of decisions about students who are influenced by their performance
on standardized tests, there is an obvious need for research on the
social implications and consequences of the widespread use of this
type of technique for assessing abilities. Toward this end Russell
Sage Foundation in 1962 initiated a program of research on the
social consequences of standardized ability testing. The aim of the
program is to assess the impact of testing on the individuals being
tested, the groups or organizations using tests, and, at the broadest
level, on the society itself. This report is one of a series of mono-
graphs presenting the findings of the research and including a discussion of implications for further studies along with policy recommendations resulting from the data. Reports of the research done
thus far have been confined primarily to the effects of educational
testing, although a national survey of public opinion regarding tests

---

[4] *Ibid.*, pp. 53–54.
[5] *Ibid.*, chap. 4.
[6] Lavin, David E., *The Prediction of Academic Performance*. Russell Sage Foundation, New York, 1965. See especially chap. 4.

has been completed[7] and a study of the use of tests in personnel selection in business and industry is currently underway.[8]

The present report deals with one aspect of the use of tests in schools, namely, the role of the teacher in testing. The teacher occupies a central role in the testing and evaluation process for a number of reasons. First, the teacher is the primary point of contact between the child and the educational system, and what teachers say and do are major influences in the process whereby the child learns to assess his own abilities. This occurs not only as a result of the instructional situation itself in which the teacher is constantly providing the pupil with evaluative feedback, but also through informal interaction in which the teacher unavoidably transmits his own general assessment of the pupil's abilities to the pupil and may actually engage in counseling with pupils. Also, teachers are more likely to be in frequent contact with parents than other school officials.

Second, the teacher very often serves as the administrator and scorer of standardized tests, especially at the elementary level where testing specialists tend to be scarcer. Even in situations where teachers are not directly involved in administering standardized tests, virtually all schools give teachers access to test scores and many schools routinely provide teachers with scores made by their pupils. Thus the teacher, in addition to being able to observe pupil performance in the classroom, has another source of estimates of his students' capabilities, one which has the added legitimacy of being derived from a standardized, objective test. One of the hypotheses with which we began our research was that this type of information about pupils would have important effects on teacher attitudes and behavior toward his students, and in many cases might actually influence evaluations of classroom performance.

Finally, in a very real sense the teacher himself is being evaluated as a consequence of the performance of his pupils on standardized achievement tests. Teachers, therefore, are not disinter-

---

[7] Preliminary findings of this study are reported in Brim, Orville G., Jr., John Neulinger, and David C. Glass, *Experiences and Attitudes of American Adults Concerning Standardized Intelligence Tests*, Technical Report No. 1 on the Social Consequences of Testing. Russell Sage Foundation, New York, 1965. Further analyses of these data will appear in a forthcoming volume by the authors, entitled *American Attitudes Toward Intelligence*, to be published by Russell Sage Foundation.

[8] This study is under the direction of Stanley H. Udy, Jr., and Vernon Buck at Yale University.

ested observers of the testing process and may be expected to make efforts to improve the performance of their pupils on standardized tests, wherever this is practical. This, in turn, results in tests having a potential impact on school curricula insofar as what is taught and how it is taught is left to the teacher.

The data presented in the following pages are concerned primarily with describing and analyzing those aspects of the teacher role having to do with testing. Chapter 2 provides data concerning the use of tests in schools generally: how many tests are given; what kinds, when, and for what purposes. It also examines school policies relating to such matters as whether teachers have access to scores, whether pupils or parents receive scores, and who is responsible for administering and scoring tests. Chapter 3 describes, from the teacher's standpoint, the extent of his contact with standardized tests and objective measurement generally. Included here are data on the amount of training teachers have had in test and measurement techniques, self-reports from teachers on their familiarity with various standardized tests, and estimates as to the frequency with which teachers participate in the testing process by serving as test administrators, scorers, and the like.

Chapter 4 provides information on teacher attitudes toward, and opinions about, standardized tests, including whether teachers think tests are accurate, fair, and useful for various purposes. These items are then examined in relation to background characteristics of teachers and such variables as the degree of their involvement in testing. Opinion items are included in the study on the assumption, to be tested, that teachers who believe that standardized tests are generally accurate and useful will tend to rely more on test scores in making decisions about pupils and in general will be more influenced in their behavior toward their pupils by tests than those teachers who feel that tests are not very useful or accurate. Data comparing teachers' opinions and attitudes with several indices of their actual use of tests including the extent to which they report scores to pupils and parents and use standardized test scores in grading pupils are presented in Chapter 5.

Chapter 6 deals with the thorny issue of coaching for tests and the consequent potential impact of standardized tests on school curricula. It includes both self-report data from teachers and data based on student responses to questions concerning the extent to which their teachers have made special efforts to prepare them for tests. Finally, Chapter 7 summarizes the implications of the data and sets forth tentative policy recommendations.

The primary source of data is a questionnaire survey of 1,450 teachers in 75 public secondary schools selected according to quota sampling procedures to represent the universe of more than 21,000 public secondary schools in the United States.[9] The data were collected by the Project Talent field staff of the American Institute for Research and analyzed according to instructions furnished by the Russell Sage Foundation research group. Although the total number of schools involved in the survey was small, considerable care was taken in sample selection and the number of individual respondents is sufficiently large to warrant a degree of confidence in the validity of the analyses based on this group of teachers.

In addition to the basic secondary school teacher sample, data were available from several other sources and wherever possible tables presented include comparisons between the responses of secondary teachers and other relevant groups. The latter include the following:

In 39 of the 75 public secondary schools surveyed extensive questionnaire data were collected from all pupils in the tenth and twelfth grades. This generated a national sample of 5,321 public secondary school students, and several questions were included in the questionnaire on such topics as whether the student had ever received reports of how well he had done on standardized tests taken in school and, if so, from whom he had received them (teachers constituting one response category); whether the student's teachers had ever made efforts specifically to prepare him for standardized tests; and whether the student felt that tests were accurate and fair. In most cases the questions asked were comparable to those asked on the Teachers' Questionnaire[10] and comparisons between student and teacher perceptions of standardized tests and testing are often enlightening.

In all 75 public secondary schools questionnaires were admin-

---

[9] A detailed description of sampling and data collection procedures appears in Appendix I. The Teachers' Questionnaire is reproduced in Appendix II.
[10] A copy of the Students' Questionnaire may be found in Brim, Orville G., Jr., David A. Goslin, David C. Glass, and Isadore Goldberg, *The Use of Standardized Ability Tests in American Secondary Schools and Their Impact on Students, Teachers, and Administrators*, Technical Report No. 3 on the Social Consequences of Testing. Russell Sage Foundation, New York, 1965, Appendix A.

istered to all school personnel formally engaged in counseling activities with students. Completed questionnaires were received from 143 counselors (all of those eligible in the schools), and their responses are included for comparative purposes where the questions asked of both teachers and counselors were the same.[11] Although the number of schools involved is the same for both counselor and teacher reports, comparisons of percentage distributions between counselors and teachers should be interpreted with some caution because of the relatively small size of the counselor sample.

Data were also collected from students, teachers, and counselors in 10 parochial secondary schools and 9 private secondary schools. Schools in these two groups were not chosen randomly, as in the case of the public school sample, but rather purposively to reflect respective types of schools.[12] The same student and teacher questionnaires used in the public secondary schools were completed by 1,198 students and 158 teachers in the private schools, and by 2,636 students and 146 teachers in the parochial schools. Since the samples of private and parochial schools are nonrandom and small, in cases where responses of teachers and students in these schools are compared with responses of teachers and students in the public secondary school sample they should be viewed as merely indicative of possible differences or similarities. Where large differences occur, as they do in several instances, we felt justified in presenting the respective response distributions as indications of points at which further research may prove to be especially worthwhile.

School officials in each of the 75 public secondary schools, 10 parochial schools, and 9 private schools completed a Testing Program Questionnaire,[13] giving information about the use made of standardized tests in the school as well as background information on the school itself and the characteristics of the student body.

Finally, as part of a separate study of elementary school testing practices, a mail survey of over 800 public elementary schools in New York, Connecticut, and New Jersey was conducted in the spring of 1962. Questionnaire responses were received from 714 elementary principals, describing in considerable detail testing practices in

[11] A copy of the Counselors' Questionnaire appears in Appendix C to the report just cited.
[12] See Appendix I of the present volume.
[13] See Appendix III.

their schools and including several items relating to the principals' opinions about standardized tests and their use.[14] On the basis of responses to the Elementary School Testing Survey, 16 schools were selected for intensive study and a research team subsequently interviewed fifth-grade pupils in each of these schools, and collected questionnaire data from teachers, pupils, and their parents. The detailed results of this study will be reported in another monograph, but in a few cases where the same questions were asked of elementary teachers and pupils as were asked of the secondary school respondents, comparisons are included in this report. The 16 elementary schools chosen for intensive study were purposely selected to represent both high and low frequency of standardized testing, reporting and nonreporting of test scores to pupils and parents, and homogeneous versus heterogeneous grouping practices within the school, and therefore do not constitute a random sample of elementary schools in these states. Consequently, again, comparisons between responses of teachers in these schools and secondary school teachers are intended only as rough indications of differences and similarities between the respective groups as a whole and should be interpreted in this light.

The following chapters, then, present data gathered from public, private, and parochial secondary school teachers, public secondary school counselors and students, and elementary school teachers, pupils, and parents. Comparisons are made between individuals having different characteristics within the various respondent groups with respect to their behavior and opinions, as well as between the different groups. Relationships between school characteristics and teacher behaviors and opinions are also explored. In all cases results are reported as being statistically significant only in those cases where significance tests can legitimately be applied to the data, for example, where two randomly selected samples are compared or where comparisons are made within a single group of respondents.

Although the data are, for the most part, descriptive, several major themes will be discerned in the discussion that follows. The

[14] The results of this survey are reported in Goslin, David A., Roberta R. Epstein, and Barbara A. Hallock, *The Use of Standardized Tests in Elementary Schools*, Technical Report No. 2 on the Social Consequences of Testing. Russell Sage Foundation, New York, 1965.

first of these concerns the adequacy of teacher preparation for that part of the role of teachers having to do with administering and interpreting standardized tests. The question of the kind of training teachers need in order to participate in the testing process will be raised in the light of data on actual training and experience of teachers in test and measurement techniques. Second, an attempt will be made to explore, at least superficially, the amount of consistency in the opinions and attitudes held by teachers about standardized tests and their uses. It will become apparent, especially in Chapter 4, that teachers' beliefs about tests are not always consistent although certain significant relationships are apparent. For example, a belief that the abilities required to do well on a standardized test are more influenced by innate factors than by learning appears to be systematically related to positive attitudes about the accuracy and usefulness of tests.

A third theme concerns the relationship between opinions and practice. The literature of the social sciences is replete with examples of situations in which people express one belief and actually behave in a way that is contrary to their expressed opinion. In the present study similar contradictions are apparent in several instances; for example, in the case of teacher attitudes about the reporting of test scores to children and parents, and their actual behavior. Further, comparisons between a simulated behavioral measure of reliance on objective information about children (for example, test scores) and responses of teachers to questions on the amount of reliance that should be placed on test scores give evidence of discontinuity between expressed opinion and actual practice.

Finally, efforts are made to examine the relationship between school testing practices on the one hand and teacher opinions and behaviors on the other. Although our sample of schools is small, several provocative findings emerge from the data. The teacher's role in evaluation has not been defined for the most part by schools and this lack of clear-cut role expectations may account for much of the observed ambivalence on the part of teachers with respect to how they feel they should use test scores, how much they should participate in the guidance process, and the like.

It should be emphasized that for the most part this research falls into the category of an exploratory study. Questionnaire responses in many instances are a poor substitute for direct behavioral observation and, more important, the varying nature of the techniques used for selecting respondents makes firm interpretations of observed differences hazardous. Nevertheless, the data point to a number of interesting hypotheses which are, at the very least, deserving of further study.

2

The uses of
standardized tests
in schools

Tᴴɪꜱ chapter summarizes data gathered from several sources to provide a picture of standardized test use in public elementary and public, private, and parochial secondary schools. Basic information on the frequency of test use is supplemented by reports of school officials on the ways test scores are used in their schools, and data on the frequency with which scores are reported to parents and children will be analyzed. In most cases comparisons between testing program variables, such as frequency of test giving, and other characteristics of the school or community setting will be made.

By now, of course, a number of studies of the extent of testing in schools have been completed, and a good deal of information in this general area is available, ranging from impressionistic surveys such as my own earlier work[1] to the data on school testing programs gathered in connection with Project Talent[2] and the elementary

---

[1] Goslin, David A., *The Search for Ability: Standardized Testing in Social Perspective*. Russell Sage Foundation, New York, 1963.
[2] Flanagan, John C., John T. Dailey, Marion F. Shaycoft, David G. Orr, and Isadore Goldberg, *A Survey and Follow-Up Study of Educational Plans and Decisions in Relation to Aptitude Patterns: Studies of the American High School*, Cooperative Research Project No. 226. University of Pittsburgh, Pittsburgh, Pa., 1962. See chap. 8.

school testing program survey conducted by the author.[3] The present data are presented both to confirm and to extend previous studies, as well as to provide a specific frame of reference for subsequent information on teacher opinions and practices. The source of most of the data to be presented below is the Testing Program Questionnaire (see Appendix III) that was completed by the principal or guidance chief in each of the 94 public, private, and parochial secondary schools included in the study. (See Chapter 1 and Appendix I.) In addition, some of the material gathered in connection with the above-mentioned elementary school testing survey, results of several items from the Counselors' Questionnaire, and data from one or two additional sources will be included.

The extent of testing

Table 1 summarizes the responses of principals in the 75 public secondary schools included in our survey to a series of questions concerned with the frequency of administration of standardized achievement, intelligence, college-admissions, vocational-interest, and personality tests in their schools. All of the principals reported that at least some standardized tests were given in their schools. The data indicate the relatively great frequency with which tests and inventories of all types are administered in the three grades covered, although only achievement tests, group intelligence tests, multi-aptitude tests, and interest inventories appear to be given with any regularity to all pupils in a given grade.

It will be noted that no type of test is universally administered in all schools in our sample. Eleven principals (14.7 per cent) reported that standardized achievement tests were not given in grades 10, 11, and 12 in their schools; 25 (33.3 per cent) indicated that no group intelligence tests were given; and 9 (12 per cent) replied that national college-admissions tests were not given in their schools. Small town and rural schools in the South and Midwest account for virtually all of these responses, a finding which coincides with the data reported by Project Talent in 1962.[4]

---

[3] Goslin, David A., Roberta R. Epstein, and Barbara A. Hallock, *The Use of Standardized Tests in Elementary Schools,* Technical Report No. 2 on the Social Consequences of Testing. Russell Sage Foundation, New York, 1965.
[4] Flanagan, John C., and others, *op. cit.,* chap. 8.

Table 1: *Percentage of public secondary schools that report giving various types of standardized tests to pupils in grades 10, 11, and 12*

TEST GIVEN TO:	ACHIEVE-MENT TESTS	GROUP INTELLI-GENCE TESTS	NATIONAL COLLEGE-ADMISSIONS TESTS	MULTI-APTITUDE TESTS	INTEREST INVEN-TORIES	PERSONALITY INVEN-TORIES
All pupils in grade 10	54.7	32.0	2.7	20.0	20.0	8.0
All pupils in grade 11	56.0	41.3	4.0	12.0	18.7	6.7
All pupils in grade 12	30.7	16.0	13.3	12.0	22.7	5.3
Some pupils in grade 10	13.3	9.3	4.0	8.0	14.7	12.0
Some pupils in grade 11	12.0	12.0	34.7	10.7	16.0	16.0
Some pupils in grade 12	10.7	10.7	73.3	13.3	20.0	16.0
The test is not given in any grade	14.7	33.3	12.0	48.0	33.3	68.0
Total number of schools responding	(75)	(75)	(75)	(75)	(75)	(75)

Table 2: Percentage of public secondary schools that responded "yes" to the question, "Are standardized achievement tests given in grades 10, 11, and 12 in your school in one or more of the following fields?"

SUBJECT AREA	PER CENT OF SCHOOLS GIVING TEST
English Fundamentals	70.7
Reading Comprehension	77.3
Foreign Languages	10.7
Social Studies	56.0
Biological Science	42.7
Physical Science	42.7
Mathematics	65.3
Total number of schools responding	(75)

With respect to the frequency of standardized achievement test use in specific subject-matter areas, the most widely given are tests of reading comprehension, with English fundamentals, mathematics, and social studies tests also being given by more than half of the schools in the sample (Table 2). According to public secondary school principals, most twelfth-grade pupils spend on the average from one to three hours during their final year taking standardized tests given by the school and four to six hours taking tests sponsored by outside agencies (Table 3).

Table 3: Average number of hours spent by public secondary school pupils taking standardized tests during the twelfth-grade year according to school reports

AVERAGE NUMBER OF HOURS	PER CENT OF SCHOOLS	
	SCHOOL-SPONSORED TESTS	EXTERNALLY SPONSORED TESTS
1 to 3	40.0	29.9
4 to 6	34.5	49.2
7 to 12	21.8	19.5
13 or more	3.2	1.5
Number of schools	(55)	(67)
Mean number of hours	(5.5)	(5.2)

Table 4: Percentage and number of various standardized tests given in 714 public elementary schools to preschool children and children in grades kindergarten to six, by type of test[a]

| TYPE OF TEST | PRE-SCHOOL | GRADE | | | | | | | NUMBER OF TESTS GIVEN | PER CENT OF ALL TESTS |
		K	1ST	2ND	3RD	4TH	5TH	6TH		
Reading Readiness	.2 (1)	61.2 (311)	34.4 (175)	2.4 (12)	.8 (4)	.2 (1)	.4 (2)	.4 (2)	100.0 (508)	6.9
Individual Intelligence	1.5 (5)	12.0 (39)	16.3 (53)	14.5 (47)	16.6 (54)	14.2 (46)	12.9 (42)	12.0 (39)	100.0 (325)	4.4
Group Intelligence	.1 (2)	4.7 (85)	12.9 (234)	11.8 (215)	20.6 (376)	14.2 (259)	16.4 (298)	19.3 (352)	100.0 (1821)	24.6
Reading Achievement	.0 (0)	.3 (2)	14.9 (112)	20.9 (157)	24.7 (186)	11.7 (88)	10.2 (77)	17.3 (130)	100.0 (752)	10.2
Arithmetic Achievement	.0 (0)	.4 (1)	2.1 (5)	5.6 (13)	35.6 (83)	12.4 (29)	14.6 (34)	29.2 (68)	99.9 (233)	3.2
Achievement Battery	.0 (0)	.1 (3)	6.7 (183)	10.0 (275)	19.2 (527)	21.9 (600)	20.4 (559)	21.6 (591)	99.9 (2738)	37.1
Other Tests	2.3 (2)	6.8 (6)	7.9 (7)	11.4 (10)	9.1 (8)	20.4 (18)	21.6 (19)	20.4 (18)	99.9 (80)	1.2
Nonstandardized Reading Tests	.0 (0)	2.9 (27)	20.9 (193)	18.4 (170)	16.9 (156)	15.1 (139)	13.9 (128)	11.8 (109)	99.9 (922)	12.5
Total	.1 (10)	6.4 (474)	13.0 (962)	12.2 (899)	18.9 (1394)	16.0 (1180)	15.7 (1159)	17.7 (1309)	100.0 (7387)	99.9

[a] Percentages are calculated across rows in all cases except right-hand column.

Data on the extent of testing in elementary schools indicate a somewhat greater frequency of test-giving in grades kindergarten through six than at the secondary school level. Principals in a random sample of 714 elementary schools in New York, New Jersey, and Connecticut were asked to list the various types of standardized tests given in each grade in their school. Table 4 provides a tabulation of their responses by grade and type of test. Since it may be assumed that in *most* cases only one test of a particular type is given in a single grade, the frequencies within any cell are roughly equivalent to the number of schools that give such a test in that grade. Since most of the schools in our sample included all grades from kindergarten to six, we obtained an average figure of more than ten tests per school through the seven grades. It should be noted that only in the case of achievement batteries in grades 3, 4, 5, and 6 does the number of tests given approach the number of schools in the sample (714), indicating that a very high proportion of schools use achievement batteries in these grades. Only one principal reported that no standardized tests were used in his school.

Some interesting findings emerge from an inspection of Table 4. In only one grade, the first, does the number of group IQ tests reported exceed the number of achievement batteries given, emphasizing the concern of elementary schools with achievement. Eighty-five IQ tests are reported as being given in kindergarten, a figure which almost certainly corresponds closely to the number of schools giving Group IQ tests at this grade level since a school would not be likely to give more than one such test in kindergarten. Given the special problems involved in administering such tests to kindergarten children,[5] these findings raise interesting questions about the use which is made of scores resulting from preschool tests and their effect on the children involved.

Finally, the relatively infrequent use of individual IQ tests should be noted, a fact which is no doubt largely due to the lack of personnel qualified to administer and interpret such tests. A detailed description of the findings of the Elementary School Testing Survey may be found in Technical Report No. 2 on the Social Con-

---

[5] See Anastasi, Anne, *Psychological Testing*, 2d ed. Macmillan Co., New York, 1961, pp. 297–300.

sequences of Testing.[6] Since a great deal of information has been accumulated about the intellectual capacities of individual students by the time they reach secondary school, the testing being done in elementary schools may have a somewhat greater impact in terms of its relative contribution to the formation of opinions on the part of school personnel about the potential of pupils. The need for initial classification and evaluation of pupils serves to explain the greater frequency of testing in the primary grades. We shall return to this point below.

The extent of testing in elementary schools is positively related to the average income level of families of children in the school and to the number of full- or part-time counselors in the school. Public elementary schools having a predominance of Protestant pupils also tend to give more tests than those that report a large Catholic enrollment. Size of elementary school does not appear to be related to amount of testing.

The small size of our sample of secondary schools does not permit detailed consideration of the relationship between extent of test-giving and school characteristics; however, several fairly clear general observations may be made. First, somewhat more testing is done in urban and suburban schools than in small town and rural schools, although size of school again does not appear to be consistently related to extent of testing. Second, schools having a high proportion of college preparatory pupils and a lower percentage of Negroes give more tests than those having fewer college preparatory students and a high proportion of Negro pupils. Finally, extent of testing is positively related to per pupil expenditures and negatively related to the percentage of male dropouts.

These data support the tentative conclusion that extensive testing is both an urban and a middle-class phenomenon, although testing is by no means restricted to urban and middle-class school situations. While existing tests may have greater validity when used in urban settings and with college preparatory pupils, members of disadvantaged groups who are likely to have more difficulty estimating their capabilities probably have a greater need for these data. The same may be said about counselors who must work with disadvan-

[6] Goslin, David A., Roberta R. Epstein, and Barbara A. Hallock, *op. cit.*

taged pupils. One could argue, therefore, that our data raise questions as to whether those pupils who most need to be tested are actually tested as much as they require.

The use made of the results

More important than the number of tests given is the use made of the results. At the outset it should be pointed out that there is no easy or very reliable way of obtaining information about how test scores are *actually* used in school settings. Reports of school principals and guidance counselors, the primary source of the data to be presented here, may be assumed to be both impressionistic and highly flavored with current philosophies about the way test scores *ought* to be used. The implication is *not* that the school officials who filled out the Testing Program Questionnaire at the secondary school level and the Elementary School Testing Survey questionnaire at the elementary level were deliberately giving a false report of their schools' policies, but merely that many schools may not have any clear-cut policy concerning the use of standardized test scores. Furthermore, it is extremely difficult for a principal to know to what extent general policies with respect to tests, if they exist, are carried out by guidance counselors, teachers, and other school personnel.

The combination of lack of policy and uncertainty about the congruence between policy and practice means that one should interpret the following data with considerable caution. While the data are clearly suggestive of the broad lines of school policy regarding tests, marked discrepancies may exist between reported policies and actual practices in many cases. Some evidence for this assumption may be seen in the reports of teachers on the way they use test scores, particularly in regard to advising pupils about their work. (See Chapter 5.)

Table 5 provides a summary of the responses of public secondary school principals to a series of items concerned with the importance of various reasons for the use of standardized tests in their school. Of greatest interest is the fact that the four reasons receiving the highest vote of importance all involve dissemination of information resulting from the test (in one form or another) to the pupil or his parents. By far the greatest importance is attributed by principals to helping pupils to gain a better understanding of their

Table 5: *Reports of public secondary school administrators of the impor-*
tance of various reasons for the use of standardized tests in their school
(Percentages)

REASONS FOR TESTING	DEGREE OF IMPORTANCE				NUMBER OF SCHOOLS RESPONDING
	OF NO IMPOR- TANCE	OF VERY LITTLE IMPOR- TANCE	FAIRLY IMPOR- TANT	VERY IMPOR- TANT	
To meet state testing requirements	54.1	17.6	13.5	14.9	(74)
To section pupils in any course by achievement level	21.3	32.0	38.7	8.0	(75)
To section pupils in any grade by level of mental ability	29.3	30.7	33.3	6.7	(75)
To help in guiding pupils into appropriate curricula	1.3	6.7	45.3	46.7	(75)
To select applicants for admission to your school	87.8	9.5	1.4	1.4	(74)
To compare the average scores of pupils with those of other schools	26.7	36.0	34.7	2.7	(75)
To measure the level of achievement of indi- viduals at the end of the school year	14.9	13.5	44.6	27.0	(74)
To measure the gain in achievement made by individuals during a school year	12.2	14.9	43.2	29.7	(74)
To measure the average gain in achievement by all pupils in a given course during the school year	12.2	35.1	31.1	21.6	(74)
To help pupils gain a better understanding of their strengths and weaknesses	1.4	1.4	25.7	71.6	(74)
To help in educational and vocational counsel- ing of pupils	1.3	.0	29.3	69.3	(75)
To help in counseling parents	1.3	12.0	40.0	46.7	(75)
To evaluate the school curriculum	2.7	18.7	49.3	29.3	(75)
To evaluate teacher effectiveness	25.3	33.3	29.3	12.0	(75)

Table 6: Reports of public secondary school administrators of the frequency with which standardized test scores are used for various purposes in their school (Percentages)

PURPOSES OF TESTING	FREQUENCY OF USE FOR THIS PURPOSE				NUMBER OF SCHOOLS RESPONDING
	NEVER	OCCASIONALLY	FREQUENTLY	VERY OFTEN	
To diagnose reasons for failure to learn on the part of pupils	5.3	25.3	41.3	28.0	(75)
To assess pupils' achievement	5.3	22.7	41.3	30.7	(75)
To provide a basis for school marks	62.7	30.7	5.3	1.3	(75)
To assess the potential learning ability of pupils	1.3	16.0	45.3	37.3	(75)
To provide a basis for individualizing instruction	9.3	48.0	32.0	10.7	(75)
To identify under- or over-achievers	1.3	24.0	44.0	30.7	(75)
To guide pupils in their choices of specific high school subjects	6.7	18.7	34.7	40.0	(75)
To guide pupils in their choices of curricula	2.7	20.0	38.7	38.7	(75)
To guide pupils in their decisions about post-high school education	.0	18.7	34.7	46.7	(75)
To guide pupils in their choices of specific colleges	10.7	36.0	24.0	29.3	(75)
To guide pupils in their choices of occupations	5.3	28.0	42.7	24.0	(75)
To inform institutions of higher learning about their applicants for admissions	5.3	20.0	29.3	45.3	(75)
To inform prospective employers about job applicants	8.0	52.0	22.7	17.3	(75)
To inform pupils about their own abilities and achievements	6.7	16.0	32.0	45.3	(75)
To inform teachers about the abilities and achievements of their pupils	1.3	21.3	41.3	36.0	(75)

Table 7: *Percentage of time various uses are reported for each type of test in 714 public elementary schools*[a]

USES OF TESTS	READING READINESS	INDIVIDUAL INTELLIGENCE	GROUP INTELLIGENCE	READING ACHIEVEMENT	ARITHMETIC ACHIEVEMENT	ACHIEVEMENT BATTERY	OTHER TESTS	NONSTANDARDIZED READING TESTS	TOTAL
Homogeneous grouping	60.8[b]	30.6	38.8	42.2	29.2	39.4	52.3	46.1	40.8
Counseling children	12.0	29.5	32.0	21.1	21.9	34.0	23.9	20.0	28.2
Grading	5.9	2.5	4.7	8.1	12.0	9.1	1.1	11.9	7.7
Evaluating the curriculum	16.9	4.6	13.9	31.9	37.3	33.1	26.1	16.9	27.6
Evaluating teachers	.8	.3	1.4	1.2	3.0	4.2	—	4.7	2.7
Diagnosing learning difficulties	55.1	70.5	59.6	77.5	78.1	78.8	79.5	77.5	71.7
Counseling parents	21.2	58.7	34.5	20.6	18.8	30.4	36.4	20.5	29.4
Other uses	7.3	17.5	9.3	5.7	4.7	3.8	13.6	5.3	6.5
Average number of uses reported	(1.8)	(2.05)	(1.95)	(2.09)	(2.06)	(2.42)	(2.37)	(2.04)	(2.15)
Total number of tests given	(508)	(325)	(1821)	(752)	(233)	(2738)	(88)	(922)	(7387)

[a] Principals could list up to four main uses for each test; consequently, percentages do not add to 100. The data are organized by test; that is, principals reported main uses for every test regularly given in their school.
[b] The largest percentage figure in each column is italicized to indicate the most frequently reported use for that particular test.

strengths and weaknesses, helping in the educational and vocational counseling of pupils, helping to counsel parents, and helping to guide pupils into appropriate curricula. No other reason for the giving of tests comes close to the percentage of principals who think that these uses are either very important and fairly important. Next most important on the list of reasons are the items concerned with measuring pupil achievement and evaluating the school's curriculum. Interestingly, despite strong feelings on the part of teachers in opposition to such a practice (see Chapter 4), evaluating teacher effectiveness is rated as either a fairly important or very important reason for testing in 41.3 per cent of the schools.

In contrast to the importance of various reasons for giving tests, Table 6 contains estimates of the *frequency* with which scores from intelligence, scholastic-aptitude, or achievement tests are used for a variety of purposes in their schools. The expected congruency between reasons for use and frequency of use is apparent in a comparison between Tables 5 and 6. In general, schools report that test scores are regularly or very often used for most of the purposes listed, and on only one item, providing a basis for school marks, do a majority of the principals indicate that test scores are never used for this purpose. As in the case of reasons for test-giving, pupil guidance appears to be the major function of school testing programs, while such potential uses of tests as grouping, grading, or adapting the curriculum to the needs of specific pupils appear to be less important.

At the elementary level a somewhat different pattern of test usage emerges although many similarities are apparent. For all of the tests covered in the Elementary School Testing Survey, diagnosing individual difficulties was the single most widely reported use (Table 7), with homogeneous grouping as the second most important use mentioned. On the other hand, counseling pupils and counseling parents are listed as uses of test scores in only a minority of the cases. Thus, while the emphasis in both elementary and secondary schools appears to be on the individual pupil, the emphasis in secondary school seems to be on guidance and the dissemination of information to the examinee, and the emphasis in elementary school is on the usefulness of test data in organizing and individualizing the curriculum of the school. There are several interpretations of ᵗhis finding.

The elementary school must deal, at the outset, with a largely undifferentiated pupil body that must be organized in the most efficacious manner for instructional purposes. The capabilities of individual pupils are unknown at the beginning and are subject to fairly rapid change during the first five or six years of schooling. During this period continual evaluation of pupil progress is necessary if the school is to make the most of its resources and provide each student with the educational experiences and opportunities he needs most. At the same time, since most children are expected to acquire generally the same set of skills in elementary school and there is little opportunity for children to choose among various educational alternatives, the guidance function of testing tends to become subordinate, while those functions relevant to increasing the effectiveness of the school take precedence.

On the other hand, by the time a student reaches secondary school a great deal of information regarding his academic capabilities has been accumulated. More choices as to type of educational experience exist, and the problem of helping students to decide among the alternatives open to them is of major importance both to the school and to the individual. Testing at the secondary school level, therefore, can be expected to be more future-oriented, with test scores playing a major role in the guidance and counseling process.

This distinction between the use of tests in elementary schools and secondary schools is far from absolute. Counseling and guidance does take place in elementary schools, and test scores are frequently an integral part of the process. In fact, the counseling that takes place at the elementary level may have a much greater impact on the formation of a child's conception of his abilities than counseling in secondary school. Many believe that it is precisely during this period of relative malleability of self-conception that more systematic information about the child's abilities (and consequently, perhaps, his possibilities for the future) should be provided. Nevertheless, our data point to a greater concern with counseling and a greater willingness to provide pupils with test scores and other information about their abilities in secondary school than in elementary school. We shall return to this point in the following section of this chapter on school policies concerning the reporting of test scores and at several points later in the book.

To provide a basis for comparisons between type of secondary school and test use, an Index of Test Use was calculated for each school on the basis of the responses to items 51–66 on the Testing Program Questionnaire,[7] concerned with the frequency of test use. Again, because of the limited size of the school sample, inferences must be drawn with care, but several interesting findings emerge from the comparative analysis. First, the observed positive relationship between an urban setting and giving more tests appears to hold for frequency of test use as well; urban schools tend to score higher on the index of frequency of test use. Second, although extent of test-giving was positively related to per pupil expenditures in our public secondary schools, extent of test *use* (as measured by the simple sum of responses on the frequency of use items) appears to be negatively related to per pupil expenditures. Thus, while high per pupil expenditure schools give more tests, they make less frequent use of them according to our data.

Finally, although the numbers are small there is evidence of a curvilinear relationship between the percentage of college-bound pupils in the school and extent of test use. The relationship is positive until one reaches a proportion of more than 75 per cent college-bound pupils, at which point schools report that tests are used *less* frequently.

In summary, while tests are *given* most in urban, high per pupil expenditure schools, they are *used* most extensively in schools having a heterogeneous student body (both college and noncollege-bound students) in which problems of pupil guidance, classification, and evaluation are likely to be more acute. Heterogeneous student body schools, as opposed to schools having a homogeneous student body (which tend to be college preparatory schools), might be expected on the average to be somewhat lower on the measure of per pupil expenditure which would account for the observed negative relationship between extent of test *use* and per pupil expenditure.

*The reporting of test scores to
pupils and parents*

While any standardized test given in a school can have a significant impact on curriculum, school organization, or on the opportu-

---

[7] See Appendix III, pp. 190–191. The Index was constructed by assigning numerical values from one (Never) to four (Very Often) to the responses to items 51–66 and then taking the simple sum of all responses to these questions.

Table 8: Public secondary school policy on the extent to which standard-ized test scores are reported to pupils and parents (Percentages)

	PER CENT OF SCHOOLS	
SCHOOL POLICY	SCHOOL-SPONSORED TESTS	EXTERNALLY SPONSORED TESTS
The results are not reported in school	4.1	8.2
Only the scores themselves are reported	9.6	5.5
Only an interpretation of the scores is reported	6.8	27.4
Both the scores themselves and an interpretation of them are reported	79.5	58.9
Number of schools	(73)	(73)

Table 9: Public secondary school counselor reports of school practices concerning the reporting of standardized test scores to parents, by type of test (Percentages)

SCHOOL POLICY	INTELLI-GENCE AND APTITUDE TESTS	STAND-ARDIZED ACHIEVE-MENT TESTS	PERSON-ALITY TESTS	VOCA-TIONAL-INTEREST TESTS
Scores are routinely sent to parents in written form	3.7	24.3	.7	10.4
Scores are routinely given to parents in personal conferences	7.4	15.4	9.6	17.0
Parents may receive scores routinely at their request	12.5	23.5	11.9	29.6
Parents may receive scores only in special cases	14.7	4.4	5.2	3.7
Parents may not receive scores, but can get interpretation of the results routinely	37.5	22.8	8.9	18.5
Parents may not receive scores, and can get interpretation of the results only in special cases	15.4	6.6	6.7	5.2
Test results are not given to parents in any form	7.4	2.9	7.4	3.0
Tests are not given in this school	1.5	.0	49.6	12.6
Number of counselors	(136)	(136)	(135)	(135)

nities available to the pupils being tested, a direct effect on self-conception of ability (and consequently, motivation, aspiration level, and the like) is possible only where the student or his parents receive some feedback on test scores. A major focus of the following report, therefore, will be school policies and teacher practices concerned with the dissemination of test scores to pupils and parents. To provide a context for the analysis of the extent to which teachers are involved in providing their pupils with test information, school principals and counselors were asked to describe general school policies on this issue.

The data presented in Tables 8 and 9 show that a good deal of information about pupils' performance on standardized tests apparently does reach the pupil involved or his parents at the secondary level. In only six schools, for example, are scores on school-sponsored standardized tests (of all types) not reported in any way to pupils or parents. But only 10 per cent of the secondary school counselors in the same schools report that parents are routinely given scores on intelligence and scholastic aptitude tests either in written form or in personal conferences. These data corroborate the finding on the Testing Program Questionnaire that in only eight of the 75 public high schools in our sample do parents routinely receive information about their children's aptitudes. In most cases our data indicate such information is available to parents, but dissemination depends on the initiative of the guidance counselor, teacher, or the parents themselves. We may conclude that while secondary schools appear to be engaging in considerable dissemination of achievement score data, they remain somewhat reluctant to provide pupils and parents with aptitude and intelligence test scores except where parents ask for it or when guidance counselors feel that it would be helpful as part of the counseling process.

In elementary schools the above-mentioned tendencies to provide achievement test scores, but no IQ or aptitude scores, are even more pronounced. Data from the elementary school testing survey indicate that very little, if any, routine reporting of intelligence test scores goes on. Some routine reporting of standardized achievement test information is available on request. (See Tables 10 to 13.)

Both in secondary school and elementary school the social class composition of the student body appears to be related to policies concerning the reporting of test scores. Secondary schools with a high

Table 10: Grade vs. policy on reporting of test scores to parents in public elementary schools, by test[a] (Percentages)

POLICY ON REPORTING SCORES	K	1ST	2ND	3RD	GRADE 4TH	5TH	6TH	ALL GRADES
Scores are reported routinely	3.0	4.5	4.0	7.9	9.5	10.0	9.2	7.5
Scores are reported on request	16.2	18.5	20.4	18.7	20.0	19.2	19.6	19.2
Interpretation given on request	73.4	69.6	68.9	64.8	63.1	62.7	63.6	65.7
Completely confidential	6.1	5.9	5.1	7.2	5.6	6.6	5.6	6.1
No response	1.3	1.4	1.6	1.3	1.8	1.5	2.0	1.6
Number of tests given	(474)	(962)	(899)	(1394)	(1180)	(1159)	(1309)	(7377)

[a] Data in Tables 10 to 13 are organized by test; that is, for each test reported as being given in each grade, principals were asked to say whether scores on that test were reported or not. Consequently, the response frequency corresponds to the number of tests given, not to the number of schools, which was 714.

28

Table 11: Grade vs. policy on reporting of test scores to children in public elementary schools, by test[a] (Percentages)

POLICY ON REPORTING SCORES	K	1ST	2ND	3RD	4TH	5TH	6TH	ALL GRADES
				GRADE				
Scores are reported routinely	1.0	4.0	4.4	8.5	11.5	11.0	10.1	8.1
Scores are sometimes reported	2.1	4.6	6.3	6.2	7.1	7.3	6.8	6.1
Some interpretation is given	29.5	42.8	48.1	49.4	51.9	52.2	53.4	48.6
Completely confidential	63.5	44.8	37.9	33.6	27.5	27.7	27.8	34.6
No response	3.8	3.8	3.2	2.3	1.9	1.7	1.9	2.5
Number of tests given	(474)	(962)	(899)	(1394)	(1180)	(1159)	(1309)	(7377)

[a] See note to Table 10.

Table 12: Type of test vs. policy on reporting of test scores to parents, by test,ᵃ for all grades in 714 public elementary schools (Percentages)

POLICY ON REPORTING SCORES	READING READINESS	INDIVIDUAL INTELLIGENCE	GROUP INTELLIGENCE	READING ACHIEVEMENT	ARITHMETIC ACHIEVEMENT	ARITHMETIC ACHIEVEMENT BATTERY	OTHER TESTS	NONSTANDARDIZED READING TESTS	TOTAL
Scores are reported routinely	3.9	2.2	1.3	3.6	5.2	14.3	19.3	5.8	7.5
Scores are reported on request	17.9	10.5	8.8	24.2	27.9	21.7	25.0	28.9	19.2
Interpretation is given on request	72.4	75.4	73.3	66.1	64.4	60.1	42.0	62.5	65.7
Completely confidential	4.5	6.8	15.2	4.0	1.7	2.4	9.1	2.0	6.1
No response	1.2	5.2	1.4	2.1	.9	1.5	4.5	.8	1.6
Number of tests given	(508)	(325)	(1821)	(752)	(233)	(2738)	(88)	(922)	(7387)

ᵃ See note to Table 10.

Table 13: *Type of test vs. policy on reporting of test scores to children, by test,[a] for all grades in 714 public elementary schools (Percentages)*

POLICY ON REPORTING SCORES	READING READINESS	INDIVIDUAL INTELLIGENCE	GROUP INTELLIGENCE	READING ACHIEVEMENT	ARITHMETIC ACHIEVEMENT	ACHIEVEMENT BATTERY	OTHER TESTS	NONSTANDARDIZED READING TESTS	TOTAL
Scores are reported routinely	2.2	.3	.6	6.2	12.4	12.1	10.2	17.0	8.1
Scores are sometimes reported	3.3	.0	1.1	8.5	8.1	7.9	11.4	11.7	6.2
Some interpretation is given	36.4	32.9	39.6	56.5	57.1	56.3	54.5	46.9	48.6
Completely confidential	54.1	61.5	55.8	26.1	21.9	21.7	20.5	22.6	34.6
No response	3.9	5.2	2.9	2.7	.4	2.0	3.4	1.8	2.5
Number of tests given	(508)	(325)	(1821)	(752)	(233)	(2738)	(88)	(922)	(7387)

[a] See note to Table 10.

proportion of college-bound pupils are more likely to provide pupils or parents with scores, and principals of elementary schools in upper-income areas indicate that more reporting of scores to parents takes place (although the degree of reporting to *children* remains the same regardless of income level). Project Talent data indicate that, at the secondary school level, reporting of scores to parents is strongly related to extent of testing and extent of test use; test scores being reported considerably more often in schools that do a great deal of testing[8] and report more uses of test scores.[9]

Again, it should be emphasized that school policies may not bear very much relationship to what actually goes on in schools and we shall return to the problem of test score reporting in Chapter 5 when we discuss teacher uses of tests.

The reporting of test scores to teachers

In most of the public secondary schools in our sample, both standardized achievement and intelligence test scores are retained in an administrative office, and any teacher who wishes may look them up. In only about 10 per cent of the secondary schools surveyed are actual test scores routinely given to the teacher. This practice contrasts with the situation in elementary schools in which teachers actually receive scores about 80 per cent of the time and have free access to all scores (with the partial exception of individual IQ test scores) in the remainder of the cases.

Data will be presented in Chapter 3 on the extent to which secondary school teachers report that they actually look up their pupils' test scores and also on the extent to which teachers are involved in administering and scoring tests. It is quite clear, however, that teachers, at the very least, have the opportunity to find out scores made by their pupils on standardized tests. The impact that this has on teacher behavior is the subject of the remainder of this report.

[8] See Brim, Orville G., Jr., David A. Goslin, David C. Glass, and Isadore Goldberg, *The Use of Standardized Ability Tests in American Secondary Schools and Their Impact on Students, Teachers, and Administrators*, Technical Report No. 3 on the Social Consequences of Testing. Russell Sage Foundation, New York, 1965, Table 13, p. 269, and Table 66, p. 295.
[9] *Ibid.*, Table 67, p. 296.

3

*Experience of teachers
with tests
and testing*

Along with data on school policies concerning standardized testing, we were interested at the outset in knowing more about the amount of contact individual teachers have had with standardized tests, both in their training and in their role as teacher. This information is important not only in its own right, as an indication of the part standardized tests play in the day-to-day activities of teachers, but also as a major factor in the extent to which tests influence other aspects of the teacher role, for example, as a stimulus to modifying course content or methods.

The data presented in this chapter deal with three aspects of this topic: (1) teacher reports of formal training they have received in testing and measurement techniques, (2) reports of familiarity on the part of teachers with specific test instruments, and (3) reports of experience administering and scoring standardized tests. Responses of teachers to questions in each of these areas will also be examined in relation to background characteristics of teachers and to characteristics of the schools and school testing programs.

In succeeding chapters these data, particularly the indices of familiarity with tests and experience administering and scoring tests, will be compared with teacher opinions about tests and reports of test usage in an effort to provide a basis for inferences about the

impact of testing on teacher behavior. The demonstration, for example, of a relationship between familiarity or experience with standardized tests and teacher behavior would lead us to hypothesize
that changes in school testing programs resulting in greater teacher
contact with tests or in aspects of the curricula of teacher training
institutions concerned with measurement techniques would, in turn,
have an effect on the way teachers carry out some aspects of their
duties in the classroom.

It should be emphasized again here that the data reported for
parochial and private secondary school teachers and elementary
school teachers are based on small, nonrepresentative samples of
the respective groups of teachers, and all comparisons between
these groups and the public secondary school sample should therefore be made with great caution. Responses of parochial, private,
and elementary teachers are presented only to provide a preliminary
indication of possible differences between teachers in different types
of schools, and only where the observed differences are quite large
can they be presumed even tentatively to represent real differences.

Formal training in measurement
techniques

Table 14 indicates that slightly more than a fifth of the public
secondary school teachers surveyed had never taken a graduate or
undergraduate course in tests and measurements. An additional 27.9
per cent of the public secondary school teachers reported having
taken only one such course. Of the elementary school teachers, 24.7
per cent had never taken such a course and 85 per cent reported having taken fewer than three courses. By way of contrast, all but 4 per
cent of the public secondary school counselors in the same schools
had taken at least one course in measurement techniques and two-
thirds of them reported having taken at least three such courses.

Parochial secondary school teachers reported almost the same
degree of exposure to testing courses as public school teachers, but
the private school teachers surveyed were a different story, 63 per
cent indicating that they had never had a course in testing. Although
not an unexpected finding since private schools are more likely to
recruit teachers without formal preparation in education, it is worth
noting since this lack of exposure is reflected in the responses of

Table 14: Responses of secondary school teachers, public secondary school counselors, and elementary school teachers to the question, "Approximately how many graduate or undergraduate courses in the following general area have you had: tests and measurements (sample course titles: individual testing, analysis of the individual, psychological measurements, diagnostic testing, group tests and techniques, mental measurements, personality testing, etc.)?" (Percentages)

NUMBER OF COURSES	SECONDARY SCHOOL TEACHERS			SECONDARY SCHOOL COUNSELORS	ELEMENTARY SCHOOL TEACHERS[a]
	PUBLIC	PRIVATE	PAROCHIAL		
None	22.1	63.0	23.9	4.2	24.7
One	27.9	20.8	31.7	11.9	
					61.8
Two	23.5	9.1	17.6	19.6	
Three	15.1	4.5	12.0	22.4	
					11.2
Four	5.8	1.3	7.0	14.7	
Five or more	5.6	1.3	7.7	27.3	2.2
Number of respondents	(1440)	(154)	(142)	(143)	(89)

[a] The response categories to question 11 on the Elementary School Teacher Questionnaire were: "none," "one or two," "three or four," and "five or more."

private school teachers to a number of related questions, such as familiarity with tests and opinions about tests.

A roughly similar pattern is found in the responses of teachers and counselors in each of the several groups to a question concerned with the number of courses taken in research methods. Table 15 shows these data. Again, public and parochial secondary school teachers report roughly the same number of courses as elementary teachers, with private school teachers having had considerably less exposure.

Taking into account background characteristics of teachers as related to their having taken testing courses, our data indicate that male teachers are significantly *more* likely to report having taken such courses than females; younger *and* older teachers (as opposed to middle-aged teachers) report *less* formal training; teachers' college and school of education trained teachers report *more* courses; and majors in languages, the humanities, and the natural sciences have had *fewer* courses. As we shall see, these differences are reflected in the opinions and practices of teachers of various types.

Table 15: Responses of secondary school teachers, public secondary school counselors, and elementary school teachers to the question, "Approximately how many graduate or undergraduate courses in the following general area have you had: methods of research (sample course titles: research in education, statistical methods in education and psychology, statistics, educational statistics, methods in educational research, research design, etc.)?" (Percentages)

NUMBER OF COURSES	SECONDARY SCHOOL TEACHERS			SECONDARY SCHOOL COUNSELORS	ELEMENTARY SCHOOL TEACHERS[a]
	PUBLIC	PRIVATE	PAROCHIAL		
None	33.9	64.3	39.0	8.4	54.5
One	29.5	19.5	32.6	28.7	36.4
Two	18.6	9.1	9.9	27.3	
Three	10.0	2.6	9.2	18.9	8.0
Four	4.0	1.9	3.5	7.0	
Five or more	4.0	2.6	5.7	9.8	1.1
Number of respondents	(1433)	(154)	(141)	(143)	(88)

[a] Response categories to question 12 on the Elementary School Teacher Questionnaire were: "none," "one or two," "three or four," and "five or more."

A rather sizable proportion of public and parochial secondary school teachers, as well as a comparable group of elementary teachers, reported having attended one or more clinics or meetings intended primarily to acquaint teachers with the content, philosophy, or methodology of standardized testing (Table 16). The fact that as many as 20 to 40 per cent of teachers have taken part in such a clinic or meeting is evidence of the degree of teacher interest in testing and the salience of this activity for their role as a teacher. These figures reflect the establishment of clinics on testing and guidance procedures sponsored by the National Defense Education Act, as well as the continuing efforts of testing firms to acquaint test users with their products. As tests become more widely used and information about their use becomes more commonly available not only to teachers, but to parents as well, these percentages are likely to increase.

Notwithstanding the finding above, the relative lack of training in testing techniques evidenced by elementary school teachers deserves comment. Data from the Elementary School Testing Survey show clearly that it is the teacher in elementary schools who is responsible for administering most of the standardized tests given in the school. Furthermore, as noted in the previous chapter, elementary teachers are more likely than are secondary school teachers to receive their students' test results routinely. Although elementary school teachers do not typically have formal responsibility for interpreting test scores to pupils and parents, the mere fact that they possess test scores opens up the possibility that this information will have an influence on their attitudes toward pupils (for example, on expectations for the attainment of particular students), as well as on such things as grouping for instructional purposes within the classroom. Yet many of these teachers have never had any formal training in measurement techniques, and it may be presumed that even those who do report having taken a course or attended a meeting or clinic have had only minimal exposure to the philosophy and methodology of standardized testing. A direct implication of our data, therefore, is the need for increased emphasis on preparing elementary teachers for this important aspect of their role in the classroom.

In our sample of secondary schools no significant relationships are evident between such school variables as size or type of residential area served (urban vs. suburban vs. rural, and the like) and the proportion of teachers who report having taken courses in test-

Table 16: Responses of secondary school teachers and elementary school teachers to the question, "Have you ever attended any clinics or meetings intended primarily to acquaint teachers with the content, philosophy, or methodology of standardized testing (not counting courses taken in college or graduate school)?" (Percentages)

	SECONDARY SCHOOL TEACHERS			ELEMENTARY SCHOOL TEACHERS
RESPONSE	PUBLIC	PRIVATE	PAROCHIAL	
Yes, within the past two years	8.5	5.8	13.8	5.7
Yes, prior to the past two years	11.1	6.5	15.2	11.4
Yes, both within and prior to the past two years	3.7	6.5	10.3	8.0
Never	67.3	77.4	54.5	71.5
I don't remember	9.3	3.9	6.2	3.4
Number of respondents	(1421)	(155)	(145)	(88)

ing, with one exception. Teachers in public schools having a high proportion of children whose parents are engaged in professional occupations report significantly lower exposure to courses in tests and measurements. On the other hand, several testing program characteristics, including the use of tests to section pupils by ability, the use of tests to inform pupils of their strengths and weaknesses, the use of tests to evaluate teachers, and the overall extent of testing in the school are significantly related to teacher reports of having taken a greater number of courses. We may conclude that where more use is made of tests and more tests are given, a greater proportion of the teachers in the school will have had some formal training in testing.

Familiarity with tests

A major section of both the secondary school and elementary school teacher questionnaires was devoted to a set of questions designed to investigate the familiarity of teachers with a variety of specifically named standardized tests. A wide range of tests were mentioned, including relatively familiar tests like the College Board Scholastic Aptitude Test, and somewhat less widely known instruments such as the Bell Adjustment Inventory (a personality test) and Educational Testing Service's Sequential Tests of Educational Progress (STEP). Teachers were asked to indicate their familiarity with each test on a four-point scale, ranging from "I have never heard of the test" to "I have examined (or studied about) the test and am familiar with it." Tabulations of the responses were made separately by test; in addition, a composite index of familiarity with tests was constructed to make possible comparisons with background, behavior, and opinion data. A complete summary of the data by test may be found in Appendix IV; however, several interesting findings deserve mention here.

Of all the tests included, the Stanford-Binet Intelligence Test turned out to be most familiar to public school teachers, both elementary and secondary, despite the fact that it is an individual test which most children do not take. As one might expect, the College Board SAT, the Kuder Preference Record, and the Iowa Tests of Educational Development also received high familiarity ratings, although, surprisingly, 10 per cent of the public secondary school teachers indicated they had never heard of the SAT. Table 17 shows

Table 17: Distribution of public, private, and parochial secondary school teachers on the index of familiarity with tests (Percentages)

SCORES ON THE INDEX OF FAMILIARITY			SECONDARY SCHOOL TEACHERS		
			PUBLIC	PRIVATE	PAROCHIAL
Low Familiarity:	1st Quartile	16–27	15.3	26.8	6.6
	2nd Quartile	28–39	47.0	48.2	42.6
	3rd Quartile	40–51	30.2	19.6	38.2
High Familiarity:	4th Quartile	52–64	7.8	4.9	12.5
Number of teachers			(1320)	(141)	(136)
Mean			(37.22)	(33.86)	(40.33)

that parochial school teachers reported evidence of greater overall familiarity with tests, a finding due perhaps to the selectivity and small size of our sample of parochial schools (it will be remembered, however, that public and parochial school teachers did not differ significantly with respect to number of courses in testing). As expected, private school teachers gave evidence of significantly lower familiarity with tests.

Because of their importance to college-bound secondary school graduates, we asked several separate questions about exposure to college-entrance tests and, in particular, whether the teacher had ever had an opportunity to examine a complete copy of the SAT, the College Board Achievement Tests, the National Merit Scholarship Qualifying Test, or any of the American College Testing Program Tests. Slightly more than 16 per cent of the fourteen hundred public secondary school teachers in our sample reported that they had examined a complete copy of the SAT (their own experience in taking the SAT was specifically excluded). Somewhat higher proportions of the private and parochial school teachers and 28 per cent of the guidance counselors gave similar responses (Table 18).

These percentages are themselves fairly small, but the SAT is one of the most carefully guarded of all standardized tests. To the extent that these responses are representative of general teacher contact with the SAT, they indicate both widespread interest in the SAT and the difficulties in keeping a test like it completely secure. No doubt many of those who responded affirmatively to this question had worked in examination centers during the administration

Table 18: Responses of secondary school teachers and public secondary school counselors to the questions, "Have you ever examined a complete copy of: A. The College Board Scholastic Aptitude Test (SAT)?" B. The National Merit Scholarship Qualifying Test?" C. Any of the tests in the American College Testing Program?" (Percentages)

| | SECONDARY SCHOOL TEACHERS | | | | | | | | | SECONDARY SCHOOL COUNSELORS | | |
| | PUBLIC | | | PRIVATE | | | PAROCHIAL | | | | | |
RESPONSE	A	B	C	A	B	C	A	B	C	A	B	C
Yes, within the past two years	6.1	6.3	4.3	12.1	5.1	5.1	12.6	15.3	6.3	18.9	29.4	13.3
Yes, prior to two years ago	8.6	8.6	7.3	7.0	6.4	1.9	4.2	6.9	3.5	7.0	8.4	2.1
Yes, both within and prior to the past two years	2.0	1.9	1.4	3.8	.0	1.9	2.8	4.2	.7	2.1	16.8	3.5
I don't think so	9.8	8.0	13.0	5.7	1.9	10.9	7.7	6.9	15.4	9.1	6.3	6.3
No	70.1	73.3	68.2	70.7	85.9	75.0	71.3	65.3	70.6	62.2	39.2	72.7
I don't know	3.4	1.9	5.9	.6	.6	5.1	1.4	1.4	3.5	.7	.0	2.1
Number of respondents	(1435)	(1437)	(1430)	(157)	(156)	(156)	(143)	(144)	(143)	(143)	(143)	(143)

of the SAT and had taken advantage of this opportunity to go over the test. Obviously, having examined an old copy of the SAT is not like knowing the questions in advance, since new forms of the test are constantly being prepared. The significance of these figures lies primarily in the fact that they demonstrate the availability of means by which teachers and other school personnel may gain direct familiarity with tests. In general, the position of the College Board and Educational Testing Service, which administers the test, has been that general knowledge about their tests on the part of teachers and counselors, as well as students, is a good thing. These data merely underscore the importance of continuing to revise the instruments used.

Another interesting finding is that over half of the public secondary school teachers, 62.5 per cent of the parochial school teachers and, surprisingly, 75.2 per cent of the secondary school counselors had never taken the SAT themselves (Table 19). An additional 13.1 per cent of the public secondary school teachers were not sure, but did not think that they had ever taken the SAT. These figures are understandable in that many institutions that train teachers do not require candidates for admission to take the College Board tests. But they substantiate the conclusion that many college preparatory students probably take courses from teachers who have never had to take the SAT in the course of their own training, a fact which makes the efforts of the College Board and the Educa-

Table 19: Responses of secondary school and elementary school teachers and public secondary school counselors to the question, "Have you ever taken the SAT?" (Percentages)

	SECONDARY SCHOOL TEACHERS			SECONDARY SCHOOL COUNSELORS	ELEMENTARY SCHOOL TEACHERS
RESPONSE	PUBLIC	PRI- VATE	PARO- CHIAL		
Yes, more than once	4.1	19.7	9.0	.7	8.0
Yes, once	17.6	22.9	17.4	9.9	27.3
I don't think so	13.1	1.9	4.9	12.1	4.5
No	52.2	52.2	62.5	75.2	53.4
I don't know	13.1	3.2	6.2	2.1	6.8
Number of respondents	(1430)	(157)	(144)	(141)	(88)

tional Testing Service to acquaint teachers with characteristics of their admissions tests even more important. In this regard, we found that only 40 per cent of the public secondary school teachers in our sample had ever seen a copy of the booklet, distributed by ETS and the College Board, entitled *A Description of the College Board Scholastic Aptitude Test*, which is available to all teachers in schools in which there are pupils who take the SAT. Although 86.7 per cent of the counselors in our schools had seen the booklet (Table 20), additional effort might be made to get it into the hands of teachers who have responsibility for college-bound pupils.

In the next section we shall be concerned with teacher reports of their experience administering and scoring standardized tests. Characteristics of teachers and of the schools in which they teach will be examined in relation both to teacher familiarity with tests and to experience administering and scoring tests in a later section of this chapter.

Experience in administering tests

Contact between teachers and tests occurs when the teacher is asked to administer a test to his students. As noted before, much of a

Table 20: Responses of secondary school teachers and public secondary school counselors to the question, "Have you ever seen a copy of the booklet, 'A Description of the College Board Scholastic Aptitude Test' (published by Educational Testing Service)?" (Percentages)

	SECONDARY SCHOOL TEACHERS			SECONDARY SCHOOL COUNSELORS
RESPONSE	PUBLIC	PRIVATE	PAROCHIAL	
Yes, a copy of each year's edition is distributed to teachers in our school	2.0	29.5	23.8	20.3
Yes	39.7	54.5	47.6	66.4
No, but I have often wondered how I might get a copy	11.1	1.9	7.7	2.1
No, this is the first time I have seen a reference to the booklet	17.9	1.9	7.7	6.3
No	29.4	12.2	13.3	4.9
Number of respondents	(1426)	(156)	(143)	(143)

Table 21: Percentage of secondary school teachers and counselors and public elementary school teachers who report having personally administered various types of standardized tests since they began teaching or counseling

TYPE OF TEST	SECONDARY SCHOOL TEACHERS			SECONDARY SCHOOL COUNSELORS	ELEMENTARY SCHOOL TEACHERS
	PUBLIC	PRIVATE	PAROCHIAL		
Group Intelligence Test (e.g., Otis or Lorge-Thorndike)	26.7 (1373)	22.5 (151)	62.9 (140)	79.1 (139)	50.6 (85)
Standardized Achievement Test (e.g., Iowa Tests of Educational Development)	49.6 (1398)	23.8 (151)	72.7 (143)	90.0 (140)	73.3 (86)
Individual Intelligence Test (e.g., Stanford-Binet or Wechsler)	19.0 (1360)	17.1 (152)	41.7 (139)	32.6 (135)	23.7 (80)
Vocational-Interest Inventory (e.g., Kuder)	25.4 (1372)	8.6 (151)	56.8 (139)	85.7 (140)	—
Personality or Adjustment Inventory	12.0 (1354)	3.4 (148)	27.3 (139)	58.4 (137)	6.3 (80)
Standardized Aptitude Test (e.g., DAT)	19.9 (1357)	24.0 (150)	49.3 (140)	72.5 (138)	—

Table 22: Percentage of secondary school teachers and public secondary school counselors and elementary school teachers who are routinely responsible for administering various kinds of standardized tests

TYPE OF TEST	SECONDARY SCHOOL TEACHERS			SECONDARY SCHOOL COUNSELORS	ELEMENTARY SCHOOL TEACHERS
	PUBLIC	PRIVATE	PAROCHIAL		
Group Intelligence Test	7.2 (1388)	5.9 (152)	33.6 (137)	69.1 (136)	29.3 (75)
Standardized Achievement Test	23.5 (1402)	14.5 (152)	46.0 (139)	78.3 (138)	73.6 (87)
Individual Intelligence Test	2.7 (1386)	5.2 (153)	11.6 (138)	24.0 (129)	9.9 (71)
Vocational-Interest Inventory	5.0 (1384)	.0 (152)	19.0 (137)	55.8 (138)	—
Personality or Adjustment Inventory	1.9 (1385)	.0 (152)	6.7 (134)	21.2 (132)	1.4 (72)
Standardized Aptitude Test	7.8 (1390)	11.1 (153)	34.5 (139)	68.3 (139)	— —

teacher's familiarity with tests probably derives from this aspect of his regular duties. Roughly half of the public secondary school teachers reported having administered a standardized achievement test at least once since they began teaching. For elementary school teachers this figure was 70 per cent (Table 21). Of the public secondary school teachers nearly one-fourth (23.5 per cent) reported that they were routinely responsible for administering a standardized achievement test each year, or every other year (Table 22). Since our sample of teachers includes many who do not teach subjects in which standardized tests are normally given, these figures point to a fairly sizable degree of teacher involvement in testing. The proportions drop markedly when one considers group intelligence tests, although elementary school teachers still turn out to be heavily involved in test administration (a quarter of them being asked to administer a group intelligence test regularly). The involvement of teachers in administering other types of tests (personality, interest, and the like) appears to be minimal with a few minor exceptions.

The expected difference between public and private school teachers shows up strongly, private school teachers reporting significantly less experience in administering and scoring tests than public school teachers. Unexpectedly, however, parochial school teachers turn out to differ greatly in the opposite direction. As may be seen from Table 21, parochial school teachers report more experience in administering tests in each category, and on the overall index of experience administering and scoring,[1] outscore public and private teachers by a wide margin (Table 23). Because of the size of the sample and the small number of schools from which it is drawn, this finding must be interpreted with considerable caution. Data from the Testing Program Questionnaire (see Chapter 2) indicate that these data may reflect in part a greater use of standardized tests in parochial schools. They may also be due to the existence of a smaller number of specialized testing personnel in these schools. In any case, as we shall see in the following chapter, this greater experience on the part of parochial school teachers appears to have important consequences for their attitudes and opinions about tests.

Perhaps most significant of these findings is the fact that the

---

[1] The index of experience in administering and scoring tests was constructed by taking the simple sum of "yes" answers to questions 104–127 on the Teachers' Questionnaire. See Appendix II.

Table 23: Distribution of public, private, and parochial secondary school teachers on the index of experience in administering and scoring tests (Percentages)

			SECONDARY SCHOOL TEACHERS		
SCORES ON THE INDEX OF EXPERIENCE			PUBLIC	PRIVATE	PAROCHIAL
Low Experience:	1st Quartile	0–5	78.8	89.4	40.3
	2nd Quartile	6–11	16.9	7.0	38.8
	3rd Quartile	12–17	4.1	3.5	18.6
High Experience:	4th Quartile	18–24	.2	.0	2.3
Number of teachers			(1272)	(142)	(129)
Mean			(3.13)	(1.93)	(7.22)

least well-prepared group of teachers (see Table 14), those in elementary schools, appears to have the greatest responsibility for administering standardized tests. This is a reasonable finding since most elementary schools do not have the services of a full-time guidance or testing specialist, but it does raise some questions about what can be done to improve the competence of elementary school teachers in this area. The problem is particularly critical since improper administration procedures may contribute to the anxiety of those taking the test and recent research has indicated that the long-range effect of high test anxiety on the performance of elementary school children is cumulative and negative.[2] Although we have no data on the extent of variation in test administration practices, at elementary level, it seems likely that some variation does exist and increased sophistication in test administration procedures may be required to overcome the effects of this variation among children whose performance on tests during the first few years of school is poor.

Background in relation to teachers' familiarity and experience

The most striking thing about the results of comparisons between background characteristics of teachers and their reported familiarity and experience with tests is that except for a strong relation-

---

[2] Sarason, Seymour B., and others, *Anxiety in Elementary School Children.* John Wiley and Sons, New York, 1960.

ship between age of the teacher and experience in administering tests, the major background variables appear to be only marginally related to familiarity and experience with tests. As one might predict, teachers holding a master's degree or doctorate report more familiarity and experience with tests than those holding only a BA degree. Guidance and education majors also tend to rate higher on familiarity with tests and experience in administering and scoring tests than do teachers in the humanities and the natural sciences.

Interestingly, teaching experience and age do not seem to be related to reported familiarity with tests, although both variables bear the expected positive relationship to experience administering and scoring tests. Reported familiarity with tests, however, is related to experience in administering and scoring tests. Our index of familiarity with tests, measuring as it does knowledge of a wide variety of different standardized tests, appears to be heavily influenced by formal training in tests and measurements (Table 24).

Teachers in urban and suburban schools as well as those in larger schools score higher on the index of familiarity with tests although not on the index of experience in administering and scoring tests. In general, positive relationships exist between most of the test use items on the Testing Program Questionnaire and both the familiarity and experience indices, although these relationships do not attain significance in all cases. Specifically scores on the index

Table 24: Comparison between familiarity of public secondary school teachers with tests and reported number of courses taken in tests and measurements (Percentages)

| | NUMBER OF COURSES IN TESTS AND MEASUREMENTS | | | | |
FAMILIARITY WITH TESTS	NONE	ONE	TWO	THREE	FOUR OR MORE
Low familiarity	39.2	26.8	21.8	16.5	10.0
	29.9	29.2	26.4	20.7	16.7
	21.3	23.9	25.7	26.6	25.3
High familiarity	9.6	20.2	26.1	36.2	48.0
Number of teachers	(301)	(377)	(307)	(188)	(150)

$\chi^2 = 122.5; p < .001$

NOTE: χ^2 calculations were based on a procedure developed by Yates, Armitage, and Cochran for analyzing linear trend data and described in Maxwell, Albert E., *Analyzing Qualitative Data*, John Wiley and Sons, New York, 1961, pp. 63–71.

of familiarity correlate significantly with: (1) the use of tests to section pupils by ability, (2) the use of tests to counsel parents, (3) the use of tests to identify under- and over-achievers, (4) the use of tests to inform teachers about the abilities of their pupils, (5) the use of tests to inform pupils of their abilities, (6) the reporting of scores to parents and children, and (7) the overall index of extent of test *use*. The index of experience in administering and scoring tests correlates weakly with nearly all of the test use items, but significantly only with the overall extent of test-giving and not with the index of test use.

In summary, it would appear that although the two indices, familiarity with tests and experience in administering tests, are related to each other, they are measuring different attributes of teachers. Familiarity with tests appears to be a function of formal training in measurement and the actual use to which tests are put in the school. High scores on the index of experience in administering tests, on the other hand, appear to be the result of many years' teaching as well as the sheer extent of test *giving* in the school (as opposed to extent of test *use*).

4

The opinions of
teachers about tests

THE OPINIONS that teachers hold about tests and their use comprise a major dimension of the complex of variables influencing the way in which tests are actually used by teachers, as well as how they affect the teacher's performance of his duties. In this chapter we shall consider two distinct sets of opinions about tests: opinions about the nature of tests and the abilities they allegedly measure, and opinions about how test instruments ought to be used in schools. In our approach to the general question of the role of teachers in testing, we assumed that the attitudes and opinions held by a teacher would directly affect the teacher's use of tests, his interpretation of test scores, and, ultimately, the impact that a test might have on the student who took it. As we shall see in the following chapters, opinions and attitudes about tests do influence use, although the relationship is not so strong as we anticipated in all cases.

Besides their relationship to testing practices, teachers' opinions about tests are of considerable interest in their own right. For one thing, they provide some direct evidence of the general sophistication of teachers about tests and, consequently, of the effectiveness of efforts on the part of test publishing firms to disseminate information about standardized tests and their proper use. It is clear from the evidence presented in Chapter 3 that teachers are heavily involved in the testing process. One might predict that through this involvement teachers as a group would hold relatively homogeneous opinions about tests paralleling those of the professional testers whose role they are taking when they serve as test administrators. However, we found considerable diversity of opinion about tests. While the largest number of respondents falls into the expected categories of response to our opinion items, a surprisingly large number of teachers express beliefs divergent from the modal category. Nothing like uniformity of opinion exists among teachers, even on some of the basic questions such as the accuracy or usefulness of tests. We shall try to examine these differences of opinion in relation to background characteristics and experiences of the teacher and to suggest some possible consequences for testing practice.

The nature of tests and intelligence

In an effort to find out what teachers think about the accuracy of standardized tests and the kinds of aptitudes or abilities they measure, we asked several of the same questions that were put to students, counselors, principals, and the adults in our national sample survey. The answers teachers gave as compared to those given by other groups of respondents are of particular interest.

Accuracy

Table 25 shows the responses of public, private, and parochial secondary school teachers, public secondary school counselors, elementary teachers, and elementary principals to the question, "How accurate do you (personally) feel most standardized intelligence or aptitude tests are in measuring a student's potential?" The similarity of opinion between public elementary and secondary school teachers and elementary principals is apparent. But secondary school counselors and parochial school teachers differ sharply from the previously mentioned groups in the direction of a greater confidence in test accuracy, while private school teachers express significantly less confidence in the accuracy of tests. Here again, as in the previous chapter, we find parochial school teachers more closely resembling counselors than public school teachers while private school teachers voice a dissident opinion. One is tempted to draw the obvious conclusion that greater involvement in testing leads to greater confidence in the accuracy of the instruments being used,

Table 25: Responses of secondary school teachers, public secondary school counselors, and elementary school teachers and principals to the question, "How accurate do you (personally) feel most standardized intelligence or aptitude tests are in measuring a student's potential?" (Percentages)

OPINION	SECONDARY SCHOOL TEACHERS			SECONDARY SCHOOL COUNSELORS	ELEMENTARY SCHOOL	
	PUBLIC	PRIVATE	PAROCHIAL		TEACHERS	PRINCIPALS
Much better than other measures of ability (e.g., teacher evaluations, nonstandardized tests)	24.8	14.9	39.2	42.7	21.1	21.1
Slightly better than other measures	44.2	39.0	37.1	42.0	47.8	48.3
No better than other measures	20.1	25.3	12.6	13.3	16.7	23.1
Not so good as other measures	4.3	9.1	6.3	1.4	5.6	1.5
Much worse than other measures	.7	.6	.0	.0	1.1	—
No opinion	6.0	11.0	4.9	.7	5.6	—
No response	—	—	—	—	2.2	5.9
Number of respondents	(1438)	(154)	(143)	(143)	(90)	(714)

Table 26: *Responses of secondary school teachers, public secondary school counselors, and elementary school teachers to the question, "Which one of the following kinds of information do you feel provides the* SINGLE MOST ACCURATE *measure of a student's intellectual ability?" (Percentages)*

MEASURES	SECONDARY SCHOOL TEACHERS			SECONDARY SCHOOL COUNSELORS	ELEMENTARY SCHOOL TEACHERS
	PUBLIC	PRIVATE	PAROCHIAL		
Grade average	14.8	15.9	15.9	15.4	8.0
Parent opinion	.2	.0	.7	.0	.0
Standardized achievement test scores	27.4	11.9	22.8	17.5	12.6
Intelligence or scholastic aptitude test scores	38.3	37.7	42.1	56.6	47.1
Teacher opinion	18.0	32.5	17.2	9.8	31.0
Student's own opinion of his ability	.8	.7	.7	.0	.0
Peer opinion	.5	1.3	.7	.7	1.1
Number of respondents	(1425)	(151)	(145)	(143)	(87)

but this hypothesis is not supported by comparisons between the index of familiarity with tests and the index of experience administering and scoring tests and opinions about the accuracy of tests (see below).

The second observation which may be made from these data is the somewhat surprising (in the light of rumored hostility to tests) degree of acceptance by all groups of the accuracy of tests. In no group do more than 10 per cent of the respondents think that standardized tests are less accurate than other measures of a student's potential (that is, teacher evaluations, grades, and the like). Actually, a majority feel that tests are better indicators than other measures.

This acceptance of objective tests, and especially intelligence tests, as the most accurate measure of intellectual potential is strikingly reflected in the responses to a question asking teachers and others to select the best measures of an individual's potential from a list that included grade average, achievement test scores, intelligence test scores, teacher evaluations, parent opinions, and others. These data are summarized in Table 26. Again, counselors, followed this time by elementary and parochial school teachers, evidence the greatest confidence in objective tests. Interestingly, the vote for grade average as the best indicator of intellectual potential is relatively light, although the combined categories of teacher opinions and grade average account for a significant percentage of the responses, especially from the private school teachers.

Data from the Students' Questionnaire, from the national adult survey, and from a questionnaire administered to parents of elementary school students indicate that standardized test scores—both achievement and intelligence tests—account for only a small proportion of personal estimates of intellectual capacity (Table 27). Only about 15 per cent of the public secondary school students

Table 27: Responses of American adults, public, private, and parochial secondary school students and elementary school parents to the question, "What has been most important to you in deciding how intelligent you (or your children) are?" (Percentages)

SOURCES OF INFORMATION	AMERI-CAN[a] ADULTS	SECONDARY SCHOOL STUDENTS			ELEMENTARY SCHOOL PARENTS[b]
		PUBLIC	PRIVATE	PAROCHIAL	
Grade average	14.2	30.4	21.0	31.6	29.9
Standardized achievement test scores (reads College Board for secondary school students)	—	2.3	6.5	5.5	5.4
IQ or scholastic aptitude test scores	3.0	14.6	7.7	16.2	1.1
Teacher opinion	5.0	7.0	7.0	9.3	38.6
Parent opinion	4.0	4.7	8.3	4.5	—
Peer opinion	3.0	1.4	1.5	.7	—
Other evaluations	3.0	7.2	7.2	4.7	—
Individual's own opinion	11.2	—	—	—	—
Other; none of these	55.5	17.8	30.1	17.1	22.7
Don't know; never think about it; no response	1.0	14.6	10.7	10.3	2.2
Number of respondents	(1482)	(5286)	(1188)	(2623)	(184)

[a] Respondents were given a card on which were listed various ways in which people decide how intelligent they are: Question then read: A. Pick the three things from that card that have had the most effect on you in deciding how intelligent you are. B. Which of those three were most important?
[b] Question 30 on the Elementary Parents' Questionnaire read: Which source of information has been *most important* to you in deciding how intelligent your son or daughter is?

in our sample indicate, for example, that IQ or scholastic aptitude test scores had been most important to them in deciding how much intelligence they have. We are faced, then, with a situation in which teachers apparently tend to rely fairly heavily on standardized test scores in evaluating the intellectual capacity of students, while students make use of other indicators, primarily grades. No doubt this is in large part due to the fact that intelligence test scores are not widely disseminated to students (see Chapter 5), but it does underscore the point that teachers and students may be using different sources of information in the formation of ability estimates. We can only speculate that under some circumstances this may result in communication difficulties and misunderstandings between teachers and students.

With respect to the relationship between background characteristics of teachers and their opinions about tests, it is interesting to note that none of the items appears to account for more than a fragmentary part of the expressed differences of opinion. Teachers holding advanced degrees have a slightly greater tendency to express the opinion that tests are more accurate, as do teachers' college graduates and education majors. Teachers who report having taken the College Board SAT tend to be slightly more negative in their attitudes about the accuracy of tests.

Most interesting of the comparisons is the *lack* of a relationship between either of our indices designed to measure involvement in testing (index of familiarity with tests; index of experience administering and scoring tests) and opinion about accuracy. As noted above, the differences in opinion between public, private, and parochial school teachers, and secondary school counselors suggest that opinion about the accuracy of tests was partly a function of contact and familiarity with tests. At least within groups of teachers, this does not appear to be the case. We shall want to consider the implications of this point below.

Relevance of tested intelligence to
qualities necessary for success
in school and after school

In addition to opinions about the accuracy of intelligence and aptitude tests, we were interested in opinions about the relevance of the kinds of abilities measured by such tests to performance in school and in subsequent nonacademic situations. Specifically, we asked teachers how important they thought the kind of intelligence measured by intelligence tests is for success in school, in the professions (such as law or medicine), and in the business world. The responses to these items are summarized in Tables 28 and 29A and 29B.

Less than one-fourth of the teachers indicated that the abilities measured by intelligence tests are more important than most other qualities for success in school or college, while almost as many replied that these abilities are less important than others. About 10 per cent of the public school teachers and a smaller percentage of private and parochial school teachers thought that these abilities are more important than most others for success in the business world. On the other hand, a third of the public school teachers felt that tested intelligence is very important for success in the professions. This difference appears to reflect the current ideology that success in the business world depends less on intelligence than on other personality characteristics, while success in the professional world depends even more on intelligence than does academic performance, even though there is no solid evidence that intelligence makes less of a difference in business success than for success in the professional world.

Interestingly, students indicate significantly greater confidence in the importance of the abilities measured by such tests, at least for academic performance, than do teachers. In this respect they resemble secondary school counselors in their opinions, as can be seen from Table 28. Even more striking are the opinions of parents of elementary school children, the majority of whom felt that such abilities were of primary importance for school achievement (as compared to elementary school teachers, who were even more skeptical than secondary school teachers).

Again, no single background characteristic or set of characteristics of teachers bears a significant relationship to the opinions expressed, although advanced training, experience, an education major and, to some extent, number of courses in tests and measurements are slightly correlated with a belief in the greater importance of tested intelligence. Familiarity with tests and experience administering and scoring tests do not show any relationship at all to these opinions.

Table 28: *Responses of secondary school students, teachers, and counselors, and elementary school teachers and parents to the question, "How important do you feel the kind of intelligence measured by intelligence tests is for success in school or college?" (Percentages)*

OPINION	SECONDARY SCHOOL STUDENTS			SECONDARY SCHOOL TEACHERS			SECONDARY SCHOOL COUNSELORS	ELEMENTARY SCHOOL TEACHERS	ELEMENTARY SCHOOL PARENTS
	PUBLIC	PRIVATE	PAROCHIAL	PUBLIC	PRIVATE	PAROCHIAL			
It is the most important factor	7.1	1.3	4.9	.8	2.1	1.4	2.1	1.1	3.3
It is more important than most other qualities	33.4	31.7	35.1	20.2	24.3	22.1	36.2	13.3	62.5
It is about the same as other qualities	21.3	25.2	25.0	56.8	41.7	53.1	45.4	55.6	12.0
It is not so important as some other qualities	11.3	22.9	16.1	16.0	22.9	20.7	14.9	17.8	15.2
It is not important at all	4.5	8.8	4.1	1.4	.7	.0	.0	1.1	1.1
No opinion	22.5	10.2	14.8	4.8	8.3	2.8	1.4	6.7	6.0
No response	—	—	—	—	—	—	—	4.4	—
Number of respondents	(5235)	(1192)	(2610)	(1406)	(144)	(145)	(141)	(90)	(184)

Table 29A: *Responses of secondary school teachers and public secondary school counselors to the question, "How important do you feel the kind of intelligence measured by standardized tests is for success in one of the professions, such as law or medicine?" (Percentages)*

| | SECONDARY SCHOOL TEACHERS | | | SECONDARY SCHOOL |
OPINION	PUBLIC	PRIVATE	PAROCHIAL	COUNSELORS
It is the most important quality for success	3.1	2.8	2.8	2.8
It is more important than most other qualities	31.7	25.4	26.9	39.7
It is about the same in importance as most other qualities	47.3	45.1	55.9	42.6
It is less important than most other qualities	10.5	16.2	12.4	12.8
It is not important at all	1.4	1.4	.0	.0
No opinion	5.8	9.2	2.1	2.1
Number of respondents	(1403)	(142)	(145)	(141)

Table 29B: *Responses of secondary school teachers and public secondary school counselors to the question, "How important do you feel the kind of intelligence measured by standardized tests is for success in the business world?" (Percentages)*

| | SECONDARY SCHOOL TEACHERS | | | SECONDARY SCHOOL |
OPINION	PUBLIC	PRIVATE	PAROCHIAL	COUNSELORS
It is the most important quality for success	.9	1.4	1.4	2.1
It is more important than most other qualities	9.3	4.9	7.6	12.1
It is about the same in importance as most other qualities	53.7	42.3	57.6	52.5
It is less important than most other qualities	28.2	32.4	29.2	30.5
It is not important at all	2.1	6.3	1.4	.0
No opinion	5.7	12.7	2.8	2.8
Number of respondents	(1407)	(142)	(144)	(141)

Table 30: Responses of American adults, secondary school students, teachers, and counselors, and elementary school teachers and parents to the question, "Do you think intelligence tests measure the intelligence a person is born with or what he has learned?" (Percentages)

OPINION	AMERICAN ADULTS	SECONDARY SCHOOL STUDENTS			SECONDARY SCHOOL TEACHERS			SECONDARY SCHOOL COUNSELORS	ELEMENTARY SCHOOL TEACHERS	ELEMENTARY SCHOOL PARENTS
		PUBLIC	PRIVATE	PAROCHIAL	PUBLIC	PRIVATE	PAROCHIAL			
Only inborn intelligence	6.0	1.7	2.0	2.3	1.1	.7	1.4	.7	1.1	.0
Mostly inborn intelligence, but learning makes some difference	20.8	10.9	23.1	15.8	25.7	30.4	41.4	37.3	34.4	20.6
Measure inborn intelligence and learning about equally	25.7	15.9	22.9	19.6	25.7	32.4	26.9	19.7	26.7	20.1
Mostly learned knowledge, but inborn intelligence makes some difference	31.7	38.4	31.1	35.3	36.3	21.6	22.8	37.3	27.8	39.1
Only learned knowledge	13.8	12.0	4.6	9.3	3.9	.7	.7	.7	3.3	7.6
No opinion	—	17.7	10.8	14.7	7.3	14.2	6.9	4.2	3.3	12.0
Other; no response; response not applicable	2.0	—	—	—	—	—	—	—	—	.5
They don't measure intelligence at all	—	3.4	5.4	3.1	—	—	—	—	3.3	—
Number of respondents	(1482)	(5288)	(1194)	(2619)	(1393)	(144)	(142)	(142)	(90)	(184)

Genetic vs. learning components in
tested intelligence

Of all of the opinions expressed about standardized tests and the nature of the abilities measured by such tests, perhaps most critical is the belief about the extent to which these abilities are inborn as opposed to learned. A major factor in the potential influence of test scores on the recipient, whether the sponsoring agency or the examinee, is whether the abilities the score is believed to represent are perceived as basically changeable or unchangeable. Since this issue is one on which the scientific community is itself still divided,[1] we predicted the existence of great diversity of opinion on the part of all groups involved in the testing process.

This prediction is fully substantiated by our data (Table 30). Among secondary school counselors, all of whom presumably have been exposed to at least a minimum amount of training in current psychometric theory and practice, a bi-modal distribution of responses to this question was found. In general, all groups surveyed tended to lean *away* from a view of tested intelligence as being primarily inborn, although very few respondents expressed the belief that the abilities measured by tests were entirely learned.

We encountered significant differences between groups of respondents in regard to the configuration of their answers to this question. Parochial secondary school teachers and counselors were most inclined to stress the importance of innate influences on test performance, followed, in order, by elementary school teachers, private secondary school teachers, public secondary school teachers, private school students, parents of elementary school students, adults in our national sample, parochial school students, and finally, public secondary school students. The most striking differences occur between students on the one hand, and teachers and counselors on the other.

Most interesting about opinions on this issue is a strong relationship between one's belief in the importance of innate factors in test performance and in the accuracy and relevance of tests. A belief that the kinds of abilities measured by intelligence and aptitude tests is mostly inborn is strongly associated with a belief in the accuracy of standardized tests, with a high opinion of the value that

---

[1] Goslin, David A., *The Search for Ability*. Russell Sage Foundation, New York, 1963, chap. 6.

ought to be accorded test scores in a variety of possible test use situations, and with a belief that IQ tests provide the single most accurate measure of a student's potential. The tendency to lay more stress on inborn abilities is also significantly related to the opinion that the abilities measured by such tests are relevant for success in school, in professional occupations, and to a lesser degree, to success in business. We may conclude that there is some evidence in support of the contention that opinions about the accuracy of tests, their usefulness, and the origin of abilities are part of a more or less internally consistent belief system, a major component of which appears to be a belief that tests measure innate abilities to a significant extent.

As might be expected, background characteristics of teachers bear the same general lack of relationship to opinion on the contribution of inborn abilities as they do to opinion about the accuracy of tests. Teachers with a master's degree or a doctorate have a tendency to put more stress on inborn characteristics, as do teachers in the age range from forty-six to fifty, natural science majors, and those who have had more experience administering and scoring tests. None of these relationships attains significance, however; all are in part explained by variations in the percentage of responses that fall into the "no opinion" category. In general, we may conclude that on this item, as in the case of opinions about the accuracy of tests, observed differences of opinions are the result of a complex and subtle mixture of a number of variables not specifically included in our analysis. We would speculate that such things as the respondent's own ability level, his or her experiences in school or college, his family orientation, and the attitudes of significant others throughout his formative years, as well as in his present occupational situation, have much to do with the formation of beliefs about the nature of abilities and their origin. The fact that opinions on these key issues do vary significantly, and appear to be related to other attitudinal items, as well as a number of behavioral indices (see Chapter 5), indicates the importance of further research on their origin and development.

Testing practices

We also wanted to learn something about how teachers felt about the amount of testing that is going on, the way tests are being used, and how they should be used. Despite the extent of public discussion over testing and the expressions of hostility toward tests on the part of many groups, we found teachers to be accepting in their attitudes about the way tests are being used and generally not disposed to criticize. No doubt, this is in part due to the professionally defined role of the teacher as a major test user. In social-psychological terms considerable dissonance would be created for the teacher who was extremely critical of tests and who at the same time was required to participate actively in a school testing program. Thus through his or her involvement in the testing process, the teacher is necessarily recruited as an ally of testing, and this fact is reflected in a variety of the responses we received to questions concerned with test use.

The number of tests being given

Most teachers felt that about the right number of school-sponsored standardized tests were being given in their schools. Only about 8 per cent of the public secondary school teachers and only 3.4 per cent of the elementary school teachers expressed the opinion that too many tests were being given, while 11.9 per cent of the public secondary school teachers and 16.1 per cent of the elemen-

Table 31: *Responses of secondary and elementary school teachers to the question, "How do you feel about the number of school-sponsored standardized tests that are given in your school?" (Percentages)*

OPINION	SECONDARY SCHOOL TEACHERS			ELEMENTARY SCHOOL TEACHERS
	PUBLIC	PRIVATE	PAROCHIAL	
Far too few tests are given	2.5	.7	.7	3.4
Too few tests are given	11.9	2.0	9.1	16.1
About the right number of tests are given	54.7	58.0	55.9	66.7
Too many tests are given	8.2	16.0	17.5	3.4
Far too many tests are given	3.3	3.3	2.8	1.1
No opinion	19.4	20.0	14.0	9.2
Number of respondents	(1423)	(150)	(143)	(87)

tary school teachers felt that too *few* tests were being used. Although a significant number of teachers declined to express an opinion on the issue, the figures above signify a fairly sizable vote of confidence in current testing programs. Somewhat greater reservations about the extent of testing were voiced by parochial and private school teachers (and fewer tests are given in private schools), but the majority were still on the side of current practice.

Somewhat the same picture results from a question about the extent of use of test scores, although a much larger percentage of all teachers felt that *not enough* use of tests is currently being made. This appears to reflect the general testing industry feeling that while many schools give tests, much better use could be made of the resulting information about pupils.

The only qualifying evidence on this point is that when characteristics of school testing programs are compared with the opinions expressed by teachers in those schools, a significant negative relationship is found between some school indicators of extent of testing and extent of test use and teachers' opinions about the desirability of more testing. For example, in schools in which the principal

Table 32: Responses of secondary and elementary school teachers to the question, "How do you feel about the amount of use that is made of scores on school-sponsored standardized tests in your school?" (Percentages)

OPINION	SECONDARY SCHOOL TEACHERS			ELEMENTARY SCHOOL TEACHERS
	PUBLIC	PRIVATE	PAROCHIAL	
Much more use should be made of test scores	20.6	7.9	21.0	14.6
Slightly more use should be made of test scores	24.9	15.2	24.5	19.1
About the right amount of use is being made of test scores	29.0	43.7	32.2	52.8
Slightly less use should be made of test scores	3.8	6.0	5.6	5.6
Much less use should be made of test scores	2.5	3.3	2.1	1.1
No opinion	19.3	23.8	14.7	6.7
Number of respondents	(1426)	(151)	(143)	(89)

or guidance counselor reported that tests were frequently used to inform teachers about the abilities of their pupils or to inform pupils about their abilities, a *larger* (but still small in absolute terms) proportion of the teachers expressed the opinion that too many tests were being given. Thus, while many teachers reported that they would like to see more use made of test scores, when such use was actually made (according to the testing program questionnaire), greater hostility to the tests was apparently generated. It should be pointed out again, however, that these data are based on a small number of schools and that the legitimacy of statistically comparing the opinions of teachers in such a small number of schools is open to question. Also, as we indicated, the percentage shift in teacher opinion is still small as compared to the majority of teachers who continued to express general confidence in the characteristics of testing programs in their schools.

Little criticism of external testing (for example, externally sponsored college-admissions tests) was evident either, although here the proportion of teachers who had no opinion increased substantially, presumably because of lack of contact. It is clear from these data that public complaints about the amount of time students are required to spend away from their studies owing to pressures of external testing programs are grossly exaggerated, at least from the teachers' perspective.

The weight to be given test scores

One of the aims of our survey was to achieve some perspective on the opinions of teachers about the relative importance of various measures of pupil abilities, including standardized test scores, in a variety of counseling and decision-making situations involving pupils. A series of 42 items was presented on which teachers were asked to estimate on a six-point scale the amount of weight which ought to be given to intelligence test scores, standardized achievement test scores, overall grade average, personality test scores, vocational-interest inventory scores, recommendations of former teachers, and information about a student's family background for *each* of the following purposes: (1) assigning a student to an accelerated track or special class for advanced students, (2) assigning a student to a special class for slow students, (3) writing a recommendation

Table 33: *Opinions of public, private, and parochial secondary school teachers on the amount of weight to be given various pupil indicators for different purposes*

INDICATORS	ASSIGN STUDENTS TO SPECIAL CLASS (ADVANCED)	ASSIGN STUDENTS TO SPECIAL CLASS (SLOW)	WRITE RECOMMEN-DATIONS FOR COLLEGE ADMISSION OR SCHOLARSHIP	ALLOW STUDENTS TO TAKE EXTRA COURSES	COUNSEL ON OCCUPATIONAL PLANS	COUNSEL ON CHOICE OF COLLEGE
A. PUBLIC SCHOOL TEACHERS[a]—MEAN WEIGHTS[b]						
Intelligence test score	4.6	4.6	3.9	4.2	4.2	4.2
Standardized achievement test scores	4.7	4.6	4.3	4.2	4.2	4.2
Overall grade average	4.8	4.6	4.8	4.9	4.4	4.6
Personality test scores	3.0	3.2	3.6	2.9	4.3	3.6
Vocational-interest inventory scores	3.8	3.6	3.7	3.6	4.9	4.4
Recommendations of former teachers	4.9	4.5	4.2	4.3	3.9	3.8
Family background	1.9	2.0	3.7	2.0	3.2	3.9
B. PRIVATE SCHOOL TEACHERS[c]—MEAN WEIGHTS[d]						
Intelligence test score	4.5	4.3	3.6	4.0	3.8	4.2
Standardized achievement test scores	4.5	4.2	3.9	3.7	3.6	4.0
Overall grade average	4.8	4.6	4.9	5.0	4.0	4.8
Personality test scores	2.4	2.6	3.3	2.4	3.8	3.4
Vocational-interest inventory scores	2.9	2.8	3.1	2.8	4.4	3.9
Recommendations of former teachers	4.8	4.8	4.6	4.7	4.0	4.2
Family background	1.6	1.8	3.5	1.6	2.8	3.2

C. PAROCHIAL SCHOOL TEACHERS[e]—MEAN WEIGHTS[f]

Intelligence test score	4.7	4.5	4.1	4.4	4.3	4.4
Standardized achievement test scores	4.9	4.7	4.6	4.4	4.4	4.4
Overall grade average	4.5	5.0	5.0	4.7	4.7	4.8
Personality test scores	3.0	3.1	3.7	2.9	4.6	3.8
Vocational-interest inventory scores	3.9	3.7	3.8	3.6	5.1	4.7
Recommendations of former teachers	4.5	4.6	4.3	4.4	4.0	3.9
Family background	2.0	2.2	4.2	2.0	3.3	4.3

[a] Cell frequencies range from 1,412 to 1,436.
[b] Range = 1–7. Higher numbers = greater weight.
[c] Cell frequencies range from 133 to 148.
[d] Range = 1–7. Higher numbers = greater weight.
[e] Cell frequencies range from 135 to 142.
[f] Range = 1–7. Higher numbers = greater weight.

for college admission or scholarship aid, (4) allowing a student to take extra courses, (5) counseling a student on occupational plans, and (6) counseling a student about his choice of a college.

A summary of mean scores on each of the weight items is presented in Table 33A–C.[2] Several observations may be made about the mean weight scores presented in this table. First, despite the finding reported earlier that teachers felt test scores and grade average to be the most accurate indicators of a student's potential and ability, these measures did not receive the highest scores here. On the other hand, recommendations of former teachers received relatively high scores across the board and the highest weight in assigning students to advanced classes. It is not surprising to find that teachers tend to feel that their own evaluations are important and accurate assessments of their pupils' capabilities, but documentation of this fact helps to temper the previously expressed formalistic confidence in objective measures. It is clear from these findings that where teachers (or former teachers) are involved in such decisions as those given, test scores and grades may not always be the crucial factors in the outcome. Interestingly, the tendency to rely more on subjective judgments is less noticeable among parochial school teachers (Table 33–C) who tend to assign higher weights to objective factors in all cases. This fact again substantiates our view of the parochial school sample as tending to be more psychometrically oriented.

Second, it is interesting to note the high mean weight assigned to vocational interest inventory results for counseling about occupational plans. This may be due in part to a tendency for the respondents to answer questions in this section rapidly and without much thought, and to a lack of psychometric sophistication on the part of teachers. It might also be interpreted as an affirmation of the ideal that children ought to be encouraged to do what most interests them. Most research data in this area indicate that vocational-interest tests add very little to the accuracy of predicting future occupa-

---

[2] A complete record of the distribution of responses by individual items may be found in Brim, Orville G., Jr., David A. Goslin, David C. Glass, and Isadore Goldberg, *The Use of Standardized Ability Tests in American Secondary Schools and Their Impact on Students, Teachers, and Administrators*, Technical Report No. 3 on the Social Consequences of Testing. Russell Sage Foundation, New York, 1965.

tional or academic success in particular fields.[3] Yet such inventories continue to be widely used in schools. Our data point up the importance of further research on the extent to which these inventories actually influence decisions made about pupils, as well as the kind of advice and counsel given.

Finally, a striking fact about the overall distribution of mean weights is the general rationality of the picture that emerges. Predictable and sharp shifts in mean weights occur at a number of points on the table; for example, in the attention given to family background characteristics for counseling about college choice as compared with assignment to a special class. Intelligence test score weight drops sharply with respect to recommendations for college scholarship aid, while overall grade average weight is highest for allowing a pupil to take extra courses. Again, it should be emphasized that at this point we are unable to determine whether this rationality of opinion is reflected in actual practice.

In addition to analyses by individual items in the series and the calculation of mean weights for each use category, indices were computed for each of the indicator variables (for example, intelligence test weight index) and for a combination of the intelligence and achievement test items (total test weight index) covering all six of the situations presented. Weight indices were calculated by converting the scale responses into numerical values (none = 1; a very slight amount = 2, etc.; a great amount = 6) and simply summing the six (or 12 in the case of the total test weight index) scores for each indicator variable.

Table 34 summarizes the percentages of secondary school teachers who fell into each numerical quartile on each of the variables. For example, 1.3 per cent of the public school teachers, 1.4 per cent of the private school teachers, and none of the parochial school teachers were in the lowest (least weight) quartile on intelligence test score weight, while for family background weight, 30.4 per cent of the public school teachers, 47.8 per cent of the private school teachers, and 21.0 per cent of the parochial school teachers were in this quartile. Since six situations were posed for all indicators except

---

[3] Lavin, David E., *The Prediction of Academic Performance*. Russell Sage Foundation, New York, 1965, chap. 5.

Table 34: *Percentage of public, private and parochial secondary school teachers in each quartile of the distribution of scores on each of the various weight indices*

WEIGHT INDICES	FIRST (LOW) QUARTILE 6.00–12.75			SECOND QUARTILE 12.76–20.50			THIRD QUARTILE 20.60–28.25			FOURTH (HIGH) QUARTILE 28.26–36.00		
	PUBLIC	PRIVATE	PAROCHIAL	PUBLIC	PRIVATE	PAROCHIAL	PUBLIC	PRIVATE	PAROCHIAL	PUBLIC	PRIVATE	PAROCHIAL
Intelligence	1.3	1.4	.0	10.5	21.5	7.9	65.3	62.5	69.6	22.8	14.6	23.0
Achievement[a]	1.6	6.2	.0	14.7	26.5	8.8	63.0	56.6	67.2	20.7	11.0	24.1
Total test	1.4	2.8	.0	10.8	21.3	6.7	69.1	66.0	71.8	18.7	9.9	21.5
Grade average	1.1	.0	.0	3.7	3.5	1.4	47.7	50.7	41.7	47.4	45.8	56.8
Personality test	14.4	27.0	8.8	35.3	38.7	41.2	42.0	29.2	42.0	8.3	5.1	8.1
Vocational-interest	6.2	18.0	3.7	20.5	36.8	20.0	50.9	35.3	48.9	22.4	9.8	27.4
Recommendations of former teachers	2.6	2.7	.8	10.2	4.5	11.9	26.0	19.6	28.0	61.2	73.2	59.3
Family background	30.4	47.8	21.0	44.5	37.7	52.2	22.0	13.0	21.0	3.1	1.4	5.8

[a] There were seven situations given for achievement tests instead of six. "Assigning grades" was added since it is a possible use of achievement test scores although not as likely a use for the other tests. See Teachers' Questionnaire, Appendix II.

achievement test scores,[4] a weight index score between 6 and 12.75 (the first quartile range) indicates an average score of between 1 and 2 ("none" and "a very slight amount"). A weight index score falling into the fourth (highest) quartile (28.26–36.00), requires the teacher to have assigned on the average at least moderate weight for all six situations.

The greater weight attributed to recommendations of former teachers shows up even more strongly in this table. Sixty-one per cent of the public school teachers, 73.2 per cent of the private school teachers, and 59.3 per cent of the parochial school teachers were in the fourth (high weight) quartile on this item, the highest proportions of any indicator variable. Conversely, the percentage of teachers in the fourth (high weight) quartile on the three test score indices (IQ, Achievement, and Total Test Weight) is dramatically lower, and grade average weight receives the second highest vote. The picture that emerges from these data and from the estimates of the accuracy of various indicators reported earlier is that although teachers tend to take the formal position that tests (along with grades) provide the best estimate of a pupil's potential, when it comes to making use of the alternative measures available, they still have greatest confidence in their own evaluations.[5] They are not willing to disregard test scores completely, but express a clear preference for teacher recommendations and overall grade average when it comes to assigning one or two variables particularly high weight for all purposes.

Again, the extent to which *actual practice* diverges from the opinions given is not known. The actual decisions made about students are the result of a very complex blend of the various pieces of information available with the weights assigned to each piece varying in accordance with changes in their absolute values and the degree of concordance among them, as well as with individual characteristics of the teacher or counselor who is making the decisions.

---

[4] "Assigning grades" was added as a possible use of achievement test scores. Consequently, the index score range for these items is 7–42.
[5] It should be noted that teacher evaluations of pupils (recommendations of former teachers, overall grade average) may be based in part on standardized test scores. Therefore, the alternatives presented on the questionnaire are not distinct from one another in practice. Another interpretation of our data would be that teachers prefer to rely on a multi-factor indicator (for example, recommendations of former teachers) rather than a single-factor indicator, such as a test score.

Some clues to this process can be derived from the analysis of the card sort data, to be discussed in the following chapter. Comparisons with background characteristics of teachers again show the same general configuration of correlations found on the items dealing with opinions about the accuracy of tests, with a few exceptions. The amount of weight assigned to objective tests is positively related to being a female teacher, age, amount of education, teachers' college training, and the index of teaching experience. As in the case of the accuracy opinions data, these variables do not show the expected correlation with the index of familiarity with tests or with the index of experience administering and scoring tests (an exception is a slight positive correlation between the index of familiarity with tests and opinions about the weight to be given to achievement test scores in assigning children to accelerated classes, classes for slow children, and in counseling about college admission). Having taken the Scholastic Aptitude Test of the College Board is consistently *negatively* related to all test weight indices, a finding which is probably a function of type of college attended and field of specialization. (Teachers' college graduates and education majors would be less likely to have taken the SAT since it is not required at teachers' colleges and state universities.)

The use of tests to evaluate teachers

All four groups of teachers (public, private, and parochial secondary school teachers, and elementary school teachers) were asked how they felt about the use of standardized achievement test scores by school administrators for evaluating the effectiveness of teachers. Predictably, very little enthusiasm for this use of tests was expressed by teachers. As can be seen from Table 35, virtually no teachers thought that this is the best (or almost always the best) way to evaluate teacher performance, and a sizable proportion felt that tests should never be used in this manner. A somewhat greater proportion of parochial school teachers were accepting of this usage of tests (again, very possibly a result of characteristics of our sample), while elementary teachers tended to be somewhat more hostile to the idea.

Female teachers, those in the humanities, and those with higher scores on the index of familiarity with tests were more likely to feel that tests should not be used in this manner. Conversely, how-

Table 35: *Responses of secondary and elementary school teachers to the question, "How do you feel about the use of standardized achievement test scores by school administrators for evaluating the effectiveness of teachers?" (Percentages)*

OPINION	SECONDARY SCHOOL TEACHERS			ELEMENTARY SCHOOL TEACHERS
	PUBLIC	PRIVATE	PAROCHIAL	
This is almost always the best way of evaluating a teacher's effectiveness	.6	1.5	.7	.0
This is sometimes the best way of evaluating a teacher's effectiveness	19.7	21.3	30.5	11.6
This is a relatively poor way of evaluating a teacher's effectiveness	47.7	54.4	51.8	59.3
Achievement test scores should never be used to evaluate a teacher's effectiveness	31.9	22.8	17.0	29.1
Number of respondents	(1393)	(136)	(141)	(86)

ever, a belief that tests were sometimes a good way of evaluating a teacher's effectiveness was significantly related to the teacher's opinion about the accuracy of tests and his opinions about the importance of the kind of intelligence measured by tests for success in school, the professions, and business. Interestingly, teachers in schools where the principal reported that tests were, in fact, used to evaluate teacher effectiveness were significantly more likely to accept this as a legitimate function of tests! (See Table 36.)

The use of test scores in assigning grades

Most public and parochial secondary school teachers felt that the teacher ought to take into account the average intelligence level of a class when setting the passing mark in assigning grades. Private school teachers differed sharply on this point, no doubt in part because of the relative homogeneity of intelligence levels in private schools and the general lack of tracking. Evidence in support of the latter hypothesis is provided by the fact that teachers in public secondary school reporting that tests are used to group students by

Table 36: Opinions of public secondary school teachers on the use of tests to evaluate teachers' effectiveness, by school policy concerning the use of achievement tests to evaluate teachers (Percentages)

OPINION	OF NO IMPOR- TANCE	OF VERY LITTLE IMPOR- TANCE	FAIRLY IMPOR- TANT	VERY IMPOR- TANT
This is almost always the best way of evaluating a teacher's effectiveness	—	.3	1.9	—
This is sometimes the best way of evaluating a teacher's effectiveness	15.4	18.1	25.3	28.2
This is a relatively poor way of evaluating a teacher's effectiveness	51.0	49.2	45.0	42.2
Achievement test scores should never be used to evaluate a teacher's effectiveness	33.6	32.4	27.9	29.6
Number of respondents	(396)	(598)	(269)	(135)

$x^2 = 139.3$; $p < .001$ (See Note to Table 24.)

ability are significantly more likely to be in favor of considering average intelligence levels before assigning grades than teachers in schools that do not indicate grouping to be a function of testing.

Elementary teachers were asked whether they thought teachers should consider their pupils' intelligence and achievement test scores (not the average intelligence level of the class) in assigning pupils' grades. Surprisingly, there was more hostility to the idea of considering standardized achievement test scores in grading than to using intelligence test scores in grading. Forty-one per cent of the elementary teachers felt that a teacher should never consider a standardized achievement score in assigning a grade in their course, as compared to only 29 per cent who felt that teachers should never consider an intelligence test score in grading.

Providing pupils and pupils' parents
with intelligence test scores

Tables 38 A–D summarize the responses of elementary and secondary school teachers to four questions concerning their opinions about

Table 37: Responses of elementary school teachers to the questions, "Do you think that teachers should consider their pupils' intelligence test scores in assigning grades?" and "Do you think that teachers should consider their pupils' standardized achievement test scores in assigning grades in their courses?" (Percentages)

OPINION	INTELLIGENCE TEST SCORES	ACHIEVEMENT TEST SCORES
Yes, always or nearly always	3.4	6.9
Yes, frequently	22.7	12.6
Only in special cases	39.8	34.5
No, never	29.5	41.4
No opinion	4.5	4.6
Number of teachers	(88)	(87)

whether teachers should provide pupils or their parents with either specific or general information about test performances. At the outset, it is clear that most teachers feel hesitant about providing either the pupil or his parents with specific information (for example, a numerical score) except under "special circumstances." Further, almost as many public secondary school teachers (7.7 per cent) felt that a teacher should *never* give a pupil even *general* information about his intelligence as felt that teachers should give such information to *most* or *all* students.

Table 38A: Opinions of secondary and elementary school teachers on whether teachers should give a student specific information about his intelligence (Percentages)

OPINION	SECONDARY SCHOOL TEACHERS			ELEMENTARY SCHOOL TEACHERS
	PUBLIC	PRIVATE	PAROCHIAL	
Yes, to most or all students	2.1	4.5	2.1	1.1
Yes, to any who ask	6.4	7.7	5.7	2.3
Yes, to some students	2.8	1.3	5.0	1.1
Yes, to some who ask	8.7	4.5	11.3	.0
Under special circumstances	49.5	44.5	57.4	37.9
No, never	26.7	32.3	17.7	55.2
No opinion	3.8	5.2	.7	2.3
Number of teachers	(1429)	(155)	(141)	(87)

Table 38B: Opinions of secondary and elementary school teachers on whether teachers should give a student general information about his intelligence (Percentages)

OPINION	SECONDARY SCHOOL TEACHERS			ELEMENTARY SCHOOL TEACHERS
	PUBLIC	PRIVATE	PAROCHIAL	
Yes, to most or all students	8.3	7.8	21.0	10.5
Yes, to any who ask	18.3	14.9	23.1	4.7
Yes, to some students	8.0	9.1	16.1	1.2
Yes, to some who ask	19.8	18.2	17.5	9.3
Under special circumstances	37.8	37.0	21.0	54.7
No, never	7.7	13.0	1.4	15.1
No opinion	.0	.0	.0	4.7
Number of teachers	(1418)	(154)	(143)	(86)

These attitudes on the part of teachers do not appear to stem primarily from a belief that the provision of such information to pupils and parents is the function of the school counselor. Much the same distribution of responses was obtained when teachers were asked whether teachers, *or* counselors, psychologists, etc., should give secondary school students specific information concerning their intelligence (Table 39). Again, over half of the teachers felt that such information should be given only in special cases, and another

Table 38C: Opinions of secondary and elementary school teachers on whether teachers should give a pupil's parents specific information about the pupil's intelligence (Percentages)

OPINION	SECONDARY SCHOOL TEACHERS			ELEMENTARY SCHOOL TEACHERS
	PUBLIC	PRIVATE	PAROCHIAL	
Yes, to most or all parents	5.6	7.1	9.7	8.0
Yes, to any who ask	14.9	12.2	13.9	5.7
Yes, to some parents	3.7	8.3	7.6	1.1
Yes, to some who ask	15.1	19.2	16.7	14.9
Under special circumstances	41.5	34.0	41.7	54.0
No, never	16.7	16.0	9.7	13.8
No opinion	2.5	3.2	.7	2.3
Number of teachers	(1424)	(156)	(144)	(87)

Table 38D: Opinions of secondary and elementary school teachers on whether teachers should give a pupil's parents general information about the pupil's intelligence (Percentages)

OPINION	SECONDARY SCHOOL TEACHERS			ELEMENTARY SCHOOL TEACHERS
	PUBLIC	PRIVATE	PAROCHIAL	
Yes, to most or all parents	13.6	21.2	23.8	29.9
Yes, to any who ask	25.5	18.6	26.6	12.6
Yes, to some parents	8.2	10.3	19.6	5.7
Yes, to some who ask	25.2	23.7	15.4	28.7
Under special circumstances	22.3	20.5	11.9	21.8
No, never	3.6	3.8	2.1	.0
No opinion	1.5	1.9	.7	1.1
Number of teachers	(1421)	(156)	(143)	(87)

17.8 per cent of the public school teachers felt no student should ever be given specific information.

Teachers having had more formal education tended to be slightly more receptive to the idea of giving pupils general information about their intelligence, while female teachers and those having a greater familiarity with standardized tests tended to be more resistant to giving pupils specific information. In general, however, background characteristics of teachers did not relate significantly to

Table 39: Responses of secondary school teachers to the question, "Do you feel that teachers, counselors, psychologists, etc., should give high school students specific information concerning their intelligence?" (Percentages)

OPINION	SECONDARY SCHOOL TEACHERS		
	PUBLIC	PRIVATE	PAROCHIAL
All students should be given this information routinely	4.9	5.1	7.6
Most students should be given this information	18.0	16.0	18.6
Only in special cases	53.8	53.2	59.3
No student should be given this information	17.8	20.5	14.5
No opinion	5.5	5.1	.0
Number of teachers	(1422)	(156)	(145)

Table 40: Responses of secondary and elementary school teachers to the question, "Do you feel that teachers ought to have their pupils' IQ scores?" (Percentages)

OPINION	SECONDARY SCHOOL TEACHERS			ELEMENTARY SCHOOL TEACHERS
	PUBLIC	PRIVATE	PAROCHIAL	
Teachers should receive these scores routinely	27.9	35.8	45.1	56.8
Teachers should have access to these scores whenever they wish	62.0	57.6	48.6	42.1
Teachers should see these scores only under special circumstances	8.0	4.6	2.8	1.1
Teachers should never see these scores	.8	.7	.7	.0
No opinion	1.3	1.3	2.8	—
Number of teachers	(1431)	(151)	(142)	(88)

differences in attitudes on these items. Nor, surprisingly, were teachers' opinions about the accuracy of standardized tests significantly related to their feelings about giving pupils or their parents test results. On the other hand, public high school teachers who felt that the kind of intelligence measured by standardized tests was important for success in school also tended to favor giving pupils general information about their intelligence. But no relationship was found between opinion about the importance of test intelligence for success in business or the professions and providing information.

Teachers in schools in which the principal reported that test scores were used for grouping students according to their abilities were significantly *less* likely to feel that pupils ought to be given any information about their intelligence. Also, where principals reported that test scores were used in grading students, teachers were significantly *less* likely to express the opinion that parents ought to have specific information.

Despite the general resistance to giving intelligence test information to parents and pupils, nearly all teachers expressed the opinion that teachers ought to have free access to such information about their students (Table 40). Thus teachers in general tend to regard such information as privileged, with the implication, at least, that although it is an important part of the teaching process, its free dis-

Table 41: Responses of secondary school students to the question, "Do you think that high school students should be given specific results of their performance on intelligence tests?" (Percentages)

	SECONDARY SCHOOL STUDENTS		
OPINION	PUBLIC	PRIVATE	PAROCHIAL
All students should be given specific results	65.9	43.7	65.8
Only bright students should be given specific results	2.2	2.3	1.9
Only "well-adjusted" students should be given specific results	7.5	15.4	11.3
Only slow students should be given specific results	2.1	.5	1.2
No students should be given specific results	13.9	27.6	13.0
None of the above	8.3	10.5	6.7
Number of students	(5261)	(1193)	(2614)

semination to those from whom it was collected would be detrimental to many. As we shall see in the following chapter, the opinions of teachers on this matter appear to be reflected in actual practice, at least according to self-reports of the teachers themselves. We shall consider some of the implications of these findings in Chapters 5 and 7.

Most interesting about the opinions of teachers on these questions is the sharp contrast between them and the opinions held by students and their parents. Our data indicate clearly the desire on the part of both parents and student respondents to have access to test score information. For example, nearly two-thirds of the more than five thousand public secondary school students in our sample felt that either IQ scores or a percentile rank ought to be made available to them on a routine basis (Table 41). Similarly, 61 per cent of the parents of elementary school students in our sample indicated that they would like to have intelligence test information reported routinely by the school while only 2 per cent of these parents felt that the school should keep this information confidential (Table 42).

This divergence of opinion about access to test scores is representative of a growing area of conflict between the school and its clients. With increasing professionalization in the field of education and a consequent specialization of educational services in the school,

Table 42: Responses of elementary school parents to the question, "Do you feel that parents should be given specific information concerning their children's performance on intelligence tests?" (Percentages)

OPINION	ELEMENTARY SCHOOL PARENTS
Yes, routinely	61.2
Yes, on request	23.5
No, except in special cases	9.3
No, never	2.2
No opinion	3.8
Number of parents	(183)

the likelihood that parents will feel estranged from the activities of the school is increased. Access to test scores is only one of several areas in which parental uneasiness at the present situation will be expressed. But because the issues are rather clearly focused here, we may predict more and more discussion between parents and educators with respect to the issue of tests. We shall want to return to this point in the concluding chapter.

5

*The role of teacher
as test user*

IT IS virtually impossible to obtain any direct information about the extent to which teachers actually make use of standardized test scores in the performance of their duties. Even if one were able to look over a teacher's shoulder as he filled out his grade sheet or wrote recommendations to college-admissions offices or evaluated pupils' qualifications for placement in special classes, it is unlikely that one could tell what part test scores were playing in the decisions the teacher was making. Further, it is extremely doubtful that teachers themselves know in an objective way how much test scores influence their opinions of pupils.

As a result, the questionnaire data reported in this chapter must be interpreted as constituting only a very rough indication of the extent of test use by teachers. Direct questions to teachers focused on three main potential uses of test scores: in grading pupils, in advising them about their work in the teacher's course, and in providing pupils and their parents with information about their abilities. Secondary school teachers also took a "card sort test" in which they were asked to evaluate 28 hypothetical pupils' qualifications for admission to a special advanced science class. This test was given in an attempt to get inferential data about the extent to which teachers rely on subjective (for example, teachers' recommendations) as opposed

Table 43: Responses of elementary and secondary school teachers to the question, "Have you ever considered a pupil's intelligence test score in assigning him a grade in one of your classes?" (Percentages)

OPINION	SECONDARY SCHOOL TEACHERS			ELEMENTARY SCHOOL TEACHERS
	PUBLIC	PRIVATE	PAROCHIAL	
Yes, always or nearly always	.1	2.0	.7	5.8
Yes, frequently	1.6	2.0	4.1	9.3
Yes, occasionally	11.2	4.6	21.4	25.6
No, but have access to scores	77.9	79.6	64.8	52.3
No, have no access to scores	7.9	10.5	7.6	5.8
Don't know	1.3	1.3	1.4	1.2
Number of teachers	(1414)	(152)	(145)	(86)

to objective (for example, test scores) data about students in a more or less "real" situation.

The use of test scores in grading

From Tables 43 and 44 it can be seen that a relatively small proportion of teachers report that they make use of standardized test scores in grading students, and those who do, do so only occasionally. These figures probably underestimate somewhat the actual influence of test scores on the grading process since the question was very likely interpreted by most teachers as referring to explicit considera-

Table 44: Responses of secondary school teachers to the question, "Have you ever considered a pupil's college-admissions test scores as one basis for assigning him a grade in one of your classes?" (Percentages)

OPINION	SECONDARY SCHOOL TEACHERS		
	PUBLIC	PRIVATE	PAROCHIAL
Yes, always or nearly always	.1	.0	.0
Yes, frequently	.1	1.3	.7
Yes, occasionally	1.5	1.3	2.1
No, but have access to scores	66.0	83.7	75.4
No, have no access to scores	30.0	12.4	20.4
Don't know	2.3	1.3	1.4
Number of teachers	(1414)	(153)	(142)

tion and, in any case, teachers may not be aware of more subtle influences that may be operative. Nevertheless, it is clear that standardized test scores do not play a major role in influencing their decisions about the grades they give pupils.

Affirmative responses to these questions are significantly related to several background characteristics of teachers, including amount of education (those holding doctorates report more use of tests); major field of study (psychology and education majors report more use of tests); years of experience teaching (more experienced teachers indicate more use); and as one would expect, knowledge of test scores. Familiarity with tests and experience in administering and scoring tests also are positively related to reported use of tests in grading, although the relationship is not a strong one. Teachers who feel that tests are generally accurate measures of a student's potential tend to report that they use tests more in grading, as do those who score higher on the test weight indices described in the previous chapter. Beliefs that teachers ought to give pupils information about their abilities and should help to prepare students to take tests are also associated with a tendency to report using test scores in grading. Finally, teachers who hold the opinion that the abilities measured by intelligence tests are more innate than learned tend to report considering scores in grading more frequently.

The picture that emerges is that teachers who generally believe in the usefulness and accuracy of tests report that they make use of test scores more than teachers who are less confident of the value of standardized tests. These findings support our view of teachers as holding consistent beliefs regarding tests, and they provide evidence in support of the hypothesized relationship between opinion and practice. However, as we shall see, this relationship is not sustained in all cases, most significantly in the case of opinions regarding the dissemination of test score information to pupils and parents, and reported practices in this area. Further, when reported practices are compared with actual use of test scores, as measured by the card sort test, additional inconsistencies appear. We shall want to examine these inconsistencies in an effort to determine their source and implications for policies regarding testing.

Several school characteristics variables show a positive relationship to reported use of test scores in grading, including size, percentage of male dropouts, type of housing, type of community, and social

Table 45: Responses of secondary and elementary school teachers to the question, "Have you ever made use of a pupil's intelligence test score in advising him about his work in your course?" (Percentages)

USE OF INTELLIGENCE TEST SCORES	SECONDARY SCHOOL TEACHERS			ELEMENTARY SCHOOL TEACHERS
	PUBLIC	PRIVATE	PAROCHIAL	
Yes, always or nearly always	.6	1.3	3.4	5.8
Yes, frequently	10.5	18.4	31.7	22.1
Yes, occasionally	48.1	39.5	45.5	43.0
No, but have access to scores	31.3	30.3	15.2	22.1
No, have no access to scores	7.8	9.9	3.4	7.0
Don't know	1.6	.7	.7	—
Number of teachers	(1417)	(152)	(145)	(86)

class; however, differences in teacher access to test scores in the different types of schools account for most of the statistical variance. Understandably, teachers in schools in which the principal or guidance counselor reports that standardized test scores play a role in grading are significantly more likely to report using scores in this manner, a finding which lends some credence to the accuracy of school reports about the use which is made of tests.

Advising students about course work

A major rationale for the use of standardized tests in schools is to enable teachers to evaluate more accurately whether pupils are performing in accordance with their abilities and to make possible more effective counseling in situations where discrepancies occur. However, a surprisingly large percentage of teachers reported they had never used intelligence test data (even though they had access to such information) in advising students about their school work. Only 11 per cent of the public secondary school teachers reported frequent use of IQ scores in this manner.

A larger proportion of our elementary school teachers indicated that they had used intelligence test scores in counseling pupils, however, and it should be remembered that the figures shown in Table 45 probably underestimate general elementary teacher use because of the purposive inclusion in the sample of several schools that do little testing. The greater involvement of elementary teachers in counseling pupils may be explained by the fact that elementary schools normally do not have the services of full-time counselors. In addition, our sample of secondary school teachers includes physical education teachers, as well as instructors in home economics and other specialized subjects in which the teacher would be less likely to have occasion to be concerned with pupil performance in relation to aptitude or intelligence.

Given the fact that most secondary school students receive relatively little (in terms of hours per semester) formal counseling from specialists in their school, the apparent teacher neglect of this potential function represents an area for further investigation and possible policy change. It is, for example, difficult to imagine how a teacher could effectively counsel a pupil about that pupil's work in the teacher's course without taking into account some indications of the pupil's abilities and aptitudes. To the extent that teachers do engage in informal counseling with pupils, assumptions about the pupil's abilities must enter into the process. Explicit consideration of a pupil's performance record on intelligence and aptitude tests might contribute substantially in many cases to the formation of more accurate perceptions of that pupil's capabilities. While it is not being suggested here that test scores should provide the total basis for such evaluation by the teacher, somewhat greater use of objective measures may be appropriate in situations where teachers are called upon to perform an advisory or counseling function.[1]

As in the case of test score use in grading, the complex of factors that includes experience and familiarity with tests and opinions about their accuracy and usefulness is strongly related to reported uses of scores for advising students. Experience in administering and scoring tests and familiarity with tests are both significantly related to a tendency for teachers to report that they use scores for this purpose (See Tables 46 and 47). Teacher opinions about the accuracy of tests is similarly related (Table 48), as are opinions about the weights that should be given to test scores in making various decisions about pupils. As expected, teachers who have access to

---

[1] See Chapter 7 of this volume, and Goslin, David A., and David C. Glass, "The Social Effects of Standardized Testing in Elementary and Secondary Schools," paper presented at the American Sociological Association annual meetings in Miami, Florida, August, 1966; *Sociology of Education*, vol. 40, 1967, in press.

Table 46: Experience of public secondary school teachers in administering and scoring tests, by use of intelligence test scores in advising students about course work (Percentages)

USE OF INTELLIGENCE TEST SCORES	EXPERIENCE IN ADMINISTERING AND SCORING TESTS			
	LITTLE EXPERIENCE		MUCH EXPERIENCE	
Always or nearly always	1.2	.0	.8	.0
Frequently	7.4	9.4	10.9	16.6
Occasionally	40.4	49.6	53.8	56.2
No, but have access to scores	39.4	32.7	27.3	18.9
No, have no access to scores	9.2	6.8	6.7	6.8
Don't know	2.4	1.5	.4	1.5
Number of teachers	(584)	(266)	(238)	(338)

$x^2 = 30.68$; $p < .001$ (In calculating x^2, "No, have no access" and "Don't know" categories were eliminated. See also Note to Table 24.)

test scores and those who feel that they have an accurate estimate of their pupils' abilities report more use of scores in advising pupils. Finally, teachers who tend to feel that tests measure inborn abilities as much as, or more, than acquired skills are more likely to report using intelligence test scores in this manner (Table 49).

Table 47: Familiarity of public secondary school teachers with tests, by use of intelligence test scores in advising students about course work (Percentages)

USE OF INTELLIGENCE TEST SCORES	FAMILIARITY WITH TESTS			
	LITTLE FAMILIARITY		MUCH FAMILIARITY	
Always or nearly always	.7	.6	.3	.8
Frequently	3.7	8.7	10.4	18.2
Occasionally	36.4	46.9	49.0	57.3
No, but have access to scores	43.9	34.2	29.9	20.7
No, have no access to scores	12.2	8.1	7.8	2.8
Don't know	3.1	1.6	2.7	.3
Number of teachers	(294)	(322)	(335)	(363)

$x^2 = 66.04$; $p < .001$ (In calculating x^2, "No, have no access" and "Don't know" categories were eliminated. See also Note to Table 24.)

Table 48: Opinions of public secondary school teachers about accuracy of intelligence tests, by use of intelligence test scores in advising students about course work (Percentages)

USE OF INTEL-LIGENCE TEST SCORES	MUCH BETTER THAN OTHER MEASURES	SLIGHTLY BETTER	NO BETTER	NOT AS GOOD	MUCH WORSE
Always or nearly always	.9	1.0	.0	.0	.0
Frequently	14.3	9.0	11.4	8.1	.0
Occasionally	49.4	51.7	44.1	38.7	22.2
No, but have access to scores	25.7	29.7	35.2	46.8	77.8
No, have no access to scores	8.0	6.3	8.9	4.8	.0
Don't know	1.7	2.2	.4	1.6	.0
Number of teachers	(350)	(630)	(281)	(62)	(9)

$\chi^2 = 15.95$; $p < .001$ (In calculating χ^2, "No, have no access" and "Don't know" categories were eliminated. See also Note to Table 24.)

Table 49: Opinions of public secondary school teachers on whether intelligence tests measure inborn intelligence or learned knowledge, by use of intelligence test scores in advising students about course work (Percentages)

USE OF INTEL-LIGENCE TEST SCORES	ONLY INBORN	MOSTLY INBORN	EQUAL	MOSTLY LEARNED	ONLY LEARNED	NO OPINION
Always or nearly always	.0	.8	.8	.6	.0	.0
Frequently	.0	15.6	10.6	9.4	5.5	2.9
Occasionally	40.0	51.1	51.5	47.7	32.7	38.8
No, but have access to scores	40.0	24.6	29.0	33.2	49.1	41.7
No, have no access to scores	20.0	5.9	6.4	8.1	10.9	12.6
Don't know	.0	2.0	1.7	1.0	1.8	3.9
Number of teachers	(15)	(358)	(359)	(509)	(55)	(103)

$\chi^2 = 16.15$; $p < .001$ (In calculating χ^2, "No, have no access" and "Don't know" categories were eliminated. See also Note to Table 24.)

Our data show, therefore, that where standardized tests are more widely used, where teachers have access to scores, and where confidence is expressed in the general accuracy of instruments used, teachers are more likely to make use of test scores in counseling pupils. Once again, these findings lead one to the tentative hypothesis that teachers are more likely to become involved in the counseling process if they have information about their pupils and if they actively participate in the evaluation process. This point is substantiated further by significant relationships between teachers' reports that they use test scores in advising students about their work and a number of testing program variables; most important, the extent of testing, the existence of a regular guidance program in the school, and the school's report that standardized test scores are regularly used to inform teachers about the abilities of their pupils, to grade pupils, and to inform pupils about their abilities.

We should not assume without further data that because a teacher reports that he has never made use of standardized intelligence test scores in advising a pupil about work in his course that this teacher does little or no counseling of his pupils using other sources of information (or even tests for that matter). Moreover, these findings emphasize the necessity for further research on whether the availability of test score data on pupils leads to greater general teacher involvement in the counseling process, leaving aside for the moment the question of the efficacy of such involvement.

The findings reported above should also be interpreted with some caution in the light of the clear ambivalence that exists among school personnel, including teachers, in regard to the question of providing pupils or their parents with information about the pupil's intelligence or aptitudes. The consideration of intelligence test scores in counseling students involves, by implication, the necessity of imparting some information to the student about his abilities in relation to his achievement. That many teachers are reluctant to provide pupils with this kind of information (or feel that this is more properly the function of the school counselor) is apparent from the data presented in the previous chapter and the following section of this chapter. One of the most important conclusions that may be drawn from the present discussion is the need for a clear statement of policy regarding the dissemination of test scores and information resulting from test scores, both by teachers and other school personnel.

*Providing students and parents with
information about their abilities*

The extent to which test scores or information about them finds its
way back to the individual who took the test is the result of a number of factors. These include: (1) what happens to the score once
the test paper has been marked; for example, are scores placed on
the pupil's permanent record; (2) which school personnel have access to test records; (3) school policies regarding the dissemination
of information to pupils and parents; (4) interest of the examinee
or his parents in his scores; and (5) the willingness of teachers,
counselors, or the school principal to repond to requests for such information or to take the initiative in providing it. Furthermore, a
significant number of students probably find out their scores by
chance as a result of an illicit look at the class testing record on the
teacher's desk or by being chosen to serve as a messenger for a docu-
ment bearing test scores.

Obviously, the teacher is only one of several potential sources
of information about test scores. Guidance counselors and principals
frequently disseminate such information and in some cases, for example, a research program like Project Talent or the two major college entrance testing programs, the testing agency itself will be a
source of scores. Nevertheless, the pupil and his parents are likely
to have more contact with teachers than with other school personnel
and this contact occurs in a context of direct concern with the pupil's intellectual achievement. The teacher is continually providing
his students with evaluations of their performance which, along
with the information received from peers, parents, and other significant reference figures, help to shape self-conceptions of ability. As
in the case of previously discussed uses of test scores, most teachers
are probably unaware, at least in any specific sense, of the extent to
which test scores influence their attitudes toward their pupils and
their evaluations of their performance. Even in the matter of actual
dissemination of test scores to pupils, we must allow for considerable
error in teacher reports.

However, some indications of the degree to which teachers are
instrumental in the feedback process may be gathered from the data
that follow. We shall be concerned, first, with teacher access to test
scores; second, with estimates of the frequency with which teachers
provide pupils and parents with either general or specific informa-

Table 50: Responses of secondary and elementary school teachers to the question, "Have you ever known any of your pupils' intelligence test scores?" (Percentages)

KNOWN INTELLIGENCE TEST SCORES	SECONDARY SCHOOL TEACHERS			ELEMENTARY SCHOOL TEACHERS
	PUBLIC	PRIVATE	PAROCHIAL	
Routinely receive most or all scores	7.5	18.2	20.3	44.2
Have access to scores and frequently look at them	24.2	17.6	27.5	22.1
Have access to scores and occasionally look at them	50.0	42.6	38.4	22.1
Don't have access, but have known some pupils' scores	8.5	8.1	9.4	4.6
Never known any scores	8.7	10.8	4.3	7.0
Pupils don't take this test	1.1	2.7	.0	—
Number of teachers	(1387)	(148)	(138)	(86)

tion about such scores; third, with estimates of how often teachers receive requests from parents and pupils for such information; and, finally, with teacher perceptions of how accurate an idea most pupils have of their own abilities.

In the following sections, as before, primary attention is focused on intelligence tests as opposed to achievement, interest, or personality tests. In addition to limitations on the number of questions that could be asked of teachers, our data indicate that most secondary schools and many elementary schools routinely transmit achievement test scores to pupils and parents—only with measures of intelligence do major differences of opinion and practice exist.

Access to intelligence test scores

The vast majority of teachers report that they either receive intelligence test scores routinely or have free access to such information. Routine distribution of intelligence scores to teachers is considerably more common at the elementary school level according to evidence from our survey of Elementary School Testing Programs[2] and questionnaire responses from elementary teachers (Table 50). If test scores are not routinely distributed, most teachers report that they at least occasionally look at pupil records in order to find out test

[2] Goslin, David A., Roberta R. Epstein, and Roberta A. Hallock, *The Use of Standardized Tests in Elementary Schools,* Technical Report No. 2 on the Social Consequences of Testing. Russell Sage Foundation, New York, 1965.

Table 51: Responses of secondary and elementary school teachers to the question, "In general, do you feel that you have an accurate estimate of how intelligent your students are?" (Percentages)

OPINION	SECONDARY SCHOOL TEACHERS			ELEMENTARY SCHOOL TEACHERS
	PUBLIC	PRIVATE	PAROCHIAL	TEACHERS
Fairly sure I know how intelligent all of my pupils are	9.3	21.3	15.9	12.6
Fairly sure I know how intelligent most of my pupils are	68.0	68.4	80.0	72.4
Fairly sure I know how intelligent a few of my students are	19.8	9.7	4.1	12.6
Don't know	2.9	.6	.0	2.3
Number of teachers	(1426)	(155)	(145)	(87)

scores. Among secondary school teachers, routine dissemination to teachers appears to be somewhat more common in private and parochial schools, although this may again be due to the nature of the respective school samples. Less than 10 per cent of teachers in all groups (except for private schools in which the figure is 10.8 per cent) respond that they have never known any pupil's IQ scores.

Teachers also express a fair amount of confidence in their ability to estimate how much ability their pupils have, although a significant minority of teachers think they have an accurate estimate of only a few of their pupils (Table 51). The latter group may not be thinking in intelligence test terms and very likely includes a disproportionate number of teachers of nonacademic subjects. Interestingly, private secondary and elementary school teachers are more likely to say they have an accurate estimate of the abilities of a greater proportion of their pupils.

Providing pupils and their parents
with intelligence test information

Teachers were asked whether they had ever given *specific information*, for example, an actual test score, or *general information*, for example, "a general idea of where the pupil stands relative to the other pupils in his class," to either pupils or their parents. The most striking general conclusion which may be drawn from the answers to these questions is that very few teachers do either. (See Tables 52 and 53.)

Table 52: Responses of secondary and elementary school teachers to the questions, "Have you ever given a student specific information about his intelligence?" and "Have you ever given a pupil general information about his intelligence?" (Percentages)

| | SECONDARY SCHOOL TEACHERS | | | | | | ELEMENTARY SCHOOL TEACHERS | |
| | PUBLIC | | PRIVATE | | PAROCHIAL | | TEACHERS | |
GIVEN INFORMATION	SPECIFIC	GENERAL	SPECIFIC	GENERAL	SPECIFIC	GENERAL	SPECIFIC	GENERAL
To most or all of my students	1.3	3.7	1.9	3.3	1.4	6.9	8.2	8.2
To many students	1.6	5.6	1.9	5.9	2.8	20.1	.0	1.2
To some students	3.8	15.2	4.5	14.4	9.1	22.9	1.2	7.1
To a few students	5.4	22.8	7.1	23.5	9.8	29.2	.0	16.5
No, but have access to scores	81.7	47.6	72.1	44.4	74.8	20.1	83.5	63.5
No, have no access to scores	6.2	5.1	12.3	8.5	2.1	.7	7.1	3.5
Number of teachers	(1419)	(1423)	(154)	(153)	(143)	(144)	(85)	(85)

Table 53: Responses of secondary and elementary school teachers to the questions, "Have you ever given a parent specific information about his child's intelligence?" and "Have you ever given a parent general information about his child's intelligence?" (Percentages)

| | SECONDARY SCHOOL TEACHERS | | | | | | ELEMENTARY SCHOOL TEACHERS | |
| | PUBLIC | | PRIVATE | | PAROCHIAL | | | |
GIVEN INFORMATION	SPECIFIC	GENERAL	SPECIFIC	GENERAL	SPECIFIC	GENERAL	SPECIFIC	GENERAL
To most or all of the parents	.4	1.9	.0	2.6	.0	4.1	3.6	7.1
To many parents	1.3	5.6	4.6	9.7	7.7	26.2	2.4	14.1
To some parents	4.5	15.8	5.9	18.2	9.9	29.0	2.4	15.3
To a few parents	10.0	30.9	9.8	29.9	19.0	25.5	10.8	47.1
No, but have access to scores	77.4	40.8	69.3	31.8	62.7	13.8	74.7	12.9
No, have no access to scores	6.3	5.0	10.5	7.8	.7	1.4	6.0	3.5
Number of teachers	(1423)	(1429)	(153)	(154)	(142)	(145)	(83)	(85)

Nearly half of the public secondary school teachers and 60 per cent of the elementary school teachers reported *never* having given a pupil even a general idea of his intelligence. With respect to actual scores, over 80 per cent of the public secondary school teachers indicated never having given such information to a pupil. On the other hand, less than 10 per cent of the elementary and secondary public school teachers reported having given many or most of their students general information, and almost none of the secondary school teachers reported having given students specific information. (Eight per cent of the elementary school teachers indicated having given most or all of their pupils specific information, but this may be due to the purposive inclusion in the elementary sample of several schools whose principals had indicated a general school policy of reporting such information to students.) Even more interesting is the finding that 40 per cent of the public secondary school teachers reported never having given parents general information and over three-quarters of this group had never given a parent specific information.

In the light of the general belief held by people in the testing field that a major function of testing should be helping pupils to have a better understanding of their capabilities, these results raise again the question of whether teachers should be explicitly encouraged to make use of test scores in their contact with students and parents. They also emphasize the need for more data on the extent to which teachers engage in counseling with parents or pupils, and, if so, what form this counseling takes.

In examining the relationship between characteristics of teachers and reporting of test scores, several significant findings emerge. Male teachers are slightly more likely to report having given information, as are education and guidance majors. General psychometric sophistication is strongly related to having given at least general information to pupils: number of courses in tests and measurements, attendance at clinics on testing, familiarity with tests, and experience in administering and scoring tests are all positively associated with dissemination of information; the latter two variables showing particularly strong relationships. (See Tables 54 and 55.)

Teachers who think tests are accurate indicators of an individual's capabilities and that considerable weight should be given to test scores in making decisions about pupils are also more likely to

Table 54: Practice of public secondary school teachers in giving students general information about their intelligence, by familiarity with tests (Percentages)

	FAMILIARITY WITH TESTS			
PRACTICE	LITTLE FAMILIARITY		MUCH FAMILIARITY	
To most or all of my students	2.7	2.5	4.4	4.1
To many students	2.7	5.3	5.3	7.9
To some students	8.9	13.4	18.9	19.1
To a few students	19.8	22.0	24.2	27.2
No, but have access to scores	58.0	51.6	42.2	40.7
No, have no access to scores	7.8	5.3	5.0	1.9
Number of teachers	(293)	(322)	(339)	(366)

$x^2 = 31.08$; $p < .001$ (In calculating x^2, "No, have no access" category was eliminated. See also Note to Table 24.)

report having given information to students. Traditionally, many psychometricians have taken the position that intelligence test scores ought not to be given to the examinee, but these relationships indicate that greater familiarity with testing procedures and more general contact with tests lead to a greater willingness to provide

Table 55: Practice of public secondary school teachers in giving students general information about their intelligence, by experience in administering and scoring tests (Percentages)

	EXPERIENCE IN ADMINISTERING AND SCORING TESTS			
PRACTICE	LITTLE EXPERIENCE		MUCH EXPERIENCE	
To most or all of my students	3.4	2.7	3.3	5.0
To many students	3.9	5.3	5.9	8.8
To some students	10.9	15.9	20.5	18.4
To a few students	19.2	22.7	23.8	28.1
No, but have access to scores	56.0	48.9	41.8	36.5
No, have no access to scores	6.6	4.5	4.6	3.2
Number of teachers	(588)	(264)	(239)	(342)

$x^2 = 34.98$; $p < .001$ (In calculating x^2, "No, have no access" category was eliminated. See also Note to Table 24.)

Table 56: Practice of public secondary school teachers in giving students general information about their intelligence, by teacher opinions about giving students general information about their intelligence (Percentages)

PRACTICE	OPINION					
	MOST OR ALL	ANY WHO ASK	SOME ROUTINELY	SOME WHO ASK	SPECIAL CIRCUMSTANCES	NEVER
To most or all of my students	18.3	8.0	3.5	2.1	.0	.0
To many students	17.4	12.6	9.6	3.6	.9	.9
To some students	20.0	21.5	27.8	18.5	9.1	2.7
To a few students	13.9	18.4	31.3	28.1	25.4	7.3
No, but have access to scores	26.1	36.0	24.3	43.1	58.4	80.9
No, have no access to scores	4.3	3.4	3.5	4.6	6.1	8.2
Number of teachers	(115)	(261)	(115)	(281)	(539)	(110)

$x^2 = 249.57$; $p < .001$ (In calculating x^2, "No, have no access" category was eliminated. See also Note to Table 24.)

the examinee or his family with some information about his performance. No doubt confidence in the validity of the test data plays a part in this willingness; however, it is encouraging to find evidence that those teachers who have had more contact with tests have not at the same time taken an overly secretive attitude about the information thus derived.

Teachers who believe they should give pupils information are more likely to report having done so. But while the relationship between opinion and practice is a strong one, it is far from perfect. In fact, 26.1 per cent of those public secondary school teachers who expressed the opinion that *all* pupils should be given general information about their intelligence reported that they themselves had *never* given *any* pupils such information (Table 56). This finding dramatizes again the conflict over the proper role of teachers in regard to counseling pupils in general and the use of test scores in this process specifically. The lack of any clear position on the advisability of giving students information about their intelligence apparently creates a situation in which practice depends on a combination of chance factors, the motivation of pupils or their parents to find out about their test performance, and the personal relationship between the teacher and his pupils or between the counselor and his counselees.

This illustrates the point that opinions and practice are not always perfectly correlated as numerous studies have indicated previously.[3] These studies have shown conclusively that the social context in which the opinion is expressed and that in which the behavior takes place, as well as characteristics of the individual himself, have a very great influence on the correlation between opinion and behavior. In the present case, as we have pointed out, school policies regarding the giving of test scores to pupils, the degree of contact between the teachers and his pupils, and a number of similar contextual variables would appear to be crucially important. Further research designed to specify the relative contribution of each of these and other variables to the level of consistency or inconsistency is clearly indicated.

[3] See, for example: Merton, Robert K., "Discrimination and the American Creed," in MacIver, Robert M., editor, *Discrimination and National Welfare*, Institute for Religious and Social Studies, Harper and Bros., New York, 1948; Lazarsfeld, Paul F., and others, *The People's Choice*, Columbia University Press, New York, 1948; and Glaser, William A., "Intention and Voting Turnout," *American Political Science Review*, vol. 52, December, 1958, pp. 1630–1640.

Table 57A: Responses of secondary and elementary school teachers to the question, "How often do your pupils ask you for information about their abilities?" (Percentages)

| PRACTICE | SECONDARY SCHOOL TEACHERS | | | ELEMENTARY SCHOOL TEACHERS |
	PUBLIC	PRIVATE	PAROCHIAL	
Frequently	5.9	9.6	11.0	3.4
Occasionally	30.7	30.1	35.2	24.1
Rarely	47.9	46.8	46.9	59.8
Never	15.5	13.5	6.9	12.6
Number of teachers	(1422)	(156)	(145)	(87)

Requests from pupils and their parents
for test scores

Surprisingly, only a small percentage of teachers indicated that they frequently receive requests from pupils or parents for information about the pupils' abilities (Tables 57A and B). Most secondary school teachers reported receiving such requests only rarely, if at all. As might be expected, elementary school teachers reported encountering a somewhat greater frequency of interest on the part of parents about their children's scores, but in absolute terms, the interest is still slight. Parochial secondary school teachers also report more requests for information, a finding which is consistent with previously reported differences between the parochial and public school teachers in our samples. While general parental apathy about school affairs, especially for members of disadvantaged groups, is, no doubt,

Table 57B: Responses of secondary and elementary school teachers to the question, "How frequently do parents of your pupils ask you for information about their children's abilities?" (Percentages)

| PRACTICE | SECONDARY SCHOOL TEACHERS | | | ELEMENTARY SCHOOL TEACHERS |
	PUBLIC	PRIVATE	PAROCHIAL	
Frequently	6.1	14.7	15.9	17.2
Occasionally	36.9	42.3	56.6	44.8
Rarely	44.4	33.3	26.9	35.6
Never	12.6	9.6	.7	2.3
Number of teachers	(1419)	(156)	(145)	(87)

Table 58: Responses of secondary and elementary school teachers to the question, "Do you feel that your students have an accurate estimate of how intelligent they are?" (Percentages)

OPINION	SECONDARY SCHOOL TEACHERS			ELEMENTARY SCHOOL TEACHERS
	PUBLIC	PRIVATE	PAROCHIAL	
Yes, all of my students have a fairly accurate estimate	1.9	3.3	4.8	1.1
Yes, most of my students	43.5	50.7	59.3	40.2
A few of my students	38.2	33.6	26.2	29.9
No, none of my students	2.3	.7	.0	6.9
Don't know	14.1	11.8	9.7	21.8
Number of teachers	(1421)	(152)	(145)	(87)

partially responsible for this absence of interest in test scores, lack of knowledge about school testing programs and unawareness of the fact that information about their children's abilities is available to parents if they ask are also relevant factors. The initiation of a program by the school to inform parents about the kinds of information available might result in greater interest and at the same time promote greater parental involvement in school activities.

Pupil and parent knowledge of intelligence test scores

Very few teachers think that all of their pupils have an accurate estimate of their intelligence, and as may be seen from Table 58, a sizable percentage of teachers hold the opinion that only a few of their pupils have an accurate estimate. More than a third of the secondary school teachers in all three groups report that at least occasionally pupils had indicated a lack of knowledge about their intelligence to the teacher (Table 59). Similarly, only about a third of our teachers felt that most or all parents whom they have come in contact with have a good idea of how intelligent their children are. Despite this, as we have noted above, apparently few teachers feel it is their duty to try to correct this state of affairs.

Our data indicate that a great deal of information does reach pupils, however. Of those secondary school pupils who recalled hav-

Table 59: *Responses of secondary and elementary school teachers to the question, "Have you ever had a student indicate to you that he did not know how intelligent he was?" (Percentages)*

| | SECONDARY SCHOOL TEACHERS | | | ELEMENTARY SCHOOL |
OPINION	PUBLIC	PRIVATE	PAROCHIAL	TEACHERS
Frequently	3.8	4.0	6.9	5.9
Occasionally	31.0	35.8	34.5	24.7
Rarely	29.9	29.8	25.5	30.6
Never	21.2	14.6	19.3	31.8
Don't remember	14.1	15.9	13.8	7.0
Number of teachers	(1427)	(141)	(145)	(85)

ing taken an intelligence test at some time during their school career, better than 60 per cent reported having received information about their performance, and, of these, more than half received a specific test score. Twenty-three per cent of the public secondary school students reported that they had received this information from the school principal or one of their teachers, and 38.9 per cent said they received it from the school counselor. Nevertheless, there are a large group of students who have never received such information even though they have taken several intelligence or aptitude tests in school. For some of these pupils, test scores or general information might have a beneficial effect on motivation or aspiration levels by helping the individual set more realistic goals, raising his motivation level, or increasing his confidence in his own abilities. Our data clearly indicate the need for the formulation of a more rational policy for the dissemination of such information, including who should take the initiative in providing it.[4]

The card sort test

As we have pointed out, it is extremely difficult to measure teacher reliance on standardized tests directly. The data reported thus far in this chapter are confined to teachers' reports of the use they make of test scores in a variety of circumstances. The best thing that can be said about such reports is that they are "suggestive" of the way tests

[4] See Chapter 7.

are actually used and that they should be interpreted with considerable caution. Prior research indicates, in fact, that teacher evaluations of their own uses of tests are subject to considerable error.[5]

In an effort to get a somewhat more objective estimate of how much teachers rely on standardized test scores as opposed to other information about students, we asked our sample of secondary school teachers to complete a test involving judgments of hypothetical pupils on the basis of several kinds of information, including test scores, provided for each hypothetical student. A set of 28 pupil record cards was given to each teacher along with instructions for the teacher to decide whether each pupil should be allowed to enroll in a special advanced science class.[6] Each pupil record form contained spaces for information about the pupil's age; sex; personality and interest inventory scores; intelligence, achievement, and aptitude test scores; recommendations of former teachers; and the opinion of the school counselor. The instructions to the teacher noted that, as in the case of any such set of record cards, the information provided was incomplete in some cases (for example, because the pupil had been absent on the day scheduled for testing), and that in not all cases did the various pieces of information about a pupil form a consistent picture. The teacher was asked to arrive at a considered opinion, on the basis of the information available, whether the student should be permitted to take the advanced course.

In 14 of the 28 cases, there was enough agreement among the various kinds of information to make a fairly straightforward classification. On the other 14 pupil records, missing or conflicting information created a direct test of the inclination of the teacher to rely either on objective (that is, test scores) or subjective (that is, teacher or counselor comments) data. Teacher judgments on these 14 test cards were scored according to whether the teacher gave greater weight to the subjective or objective information (as determined by whether the teacher decided to place the pupil in the advanced class or not), and a total score was calculated for each teacher indicating his or her overall reliance on objective information. The scoring procedure used created a possible score range from 24 (indicating consistent judgments based on the subjective infor-

---

[5] Hastings, J. Thomas, and others, *The Use of Test Results.* Bureau of Educational Research, Urbana, Ill., 1960.
[6] See Teachers' Questionnaire, Appendix II.

Table 60: Distribution of scores of secondary school teachers on the card sort test (Percentages)

	SECONDARY SCHOOL TEACHERS		
CARD SORT TEST SCORE	PUBLIC	PRIVATE	PAROCHIAL
24 to 29	3.3	3.3	.7
30 to 39	12.4	11.2	9.9
40 to 49	19.3	21.2	11.2
50 to 59	27.0	25.1	33.2
60 to 69	23.8	20.4	27.6
70 to 79	11.5	13.9	14.8
80 to 88	2.7	4.7	2.1
Number of teachers	(1398)	(151)	(141)
Mean Score	(54.55)	(54.82)	(57.80)

mation available) to 88 (indicating consistent reliance on the objective data provided.[7]

From Table 60 it may be seen that teacher scores on the card sort test were distributed over practically the entire possible range, although, as expected, the majority of teachers obtained scores falling into the two middle quartiles. Previously observed differences in opinions and practices between public, private, and parochial school teachers show up again here, with the parochial school group giving evidence of higher reliance on the objective measure than either of the other groups.

The remainder of this section is concerned with the relation between card sort scores and: (1) teacher reports of their use of test scores in grading, counseling students, and the like; (2) background characteristics of teachers, including their experience and familiarity with tests; (3) their opinions about the tests and the way scores ought to be used; and (4) school policies regarding testing.

Card sort scores vs. teacher reports
of test score use

Assuming that the card sort test measures a generalized tendency on the part of teachers to rely on test scores as opposed to other data

[7] A detailed description of scoring and validation procedures appears in Hastings, J. Thomas, *op. cit.*

about pupils, and that teacher reports of their own use of test scores in grading, advising pupils about their work, and the like are more or less accurate, we would expect to find a high relationship between card sort scores and test-use reports. A lack of such a relationship would indicate either that reliance on test scores is highly situationally specific, that is, not a generalized characteristic of teachers, or that teachers are inaccurate in reporting the extent of their own use of test data.

The only teacher-use item that relates significantly to card sort scores is the question concerned with whether the teacher had made use of IQ test scores in advising pupils about work in their course (Table 61). Teachers who report that they have given parents general information about their children's intelligence are slightly more likely to have high card sort scores, but no clear relationship appears between teacher reports of the use of test scores in grading and the card sort test.

Apparently, then, teacher uses of test scores are to some extent contextually specific and dependent upon the kinds of alternative information available. In addition, questions are raised about the reliability of our data based on what teachers said about how much they have made use of test data in the past. Our inclination to place more faith in the validity of the card sort test as an indicator of true

Table 61: *Public secondary school teachers' use of intelligence test scores in advising pupils about work in a course, by card sort test score* (*Percentages*)

CARD SORT TEST SCORE	DON'T KNOW	NO, NO ACCESS	NO, HAVE ACCESS	OCCASION- ALLY	FREQUENTLY OR ALWAYS
24 to 29	8.3	7.8	2.3	2.8	1.9
30 to 39	12.5	15.7	12.8	11.9	10.2
40 to 49	25.0	23.5	20.6	18.6	15.9
50 to 59	20.8	25.5	29.3	25.6	31.2
60 to 69	25.0	16.7	24.0	24.8	22.3
70 to 79	8.3	7.8	8.0	13.5	16.6
80 to 88	.0	2.9	3.0	2.7	1.9
Number of teachers	(24)	(102)	(437)	(669)	(157)

$\chi^2 = 4.05$; $p < .05$ (χ^2 calculated on "no, have access," "occasionally," and "frequently or always" columns only. See also Note to Table 24.)

teacher behavior and attitudes is based on the assumption that the card sort test comes closer to requiring teachers to exhibit real behavior than a questionnaire item on which an opinion is expressed. The accuracy of this assumption may legitimately be challenged, however, and further work is clearly indicated. As we pointed out above, better ways of evaluating the extent of actual use of test scores by teachers are badly needed.

Card sort scores vs. teacher opinions
and background characteristics

The most interesting feature of the results of comparisons of background characteristics (including experience with tests and testing) and opinions about tests with card sort test scores is that very few of the relationships examined attained significance. Age, sex, type of college attended, major field, and amount of experience teaching do not appear to be strongly related to a tendency to rely heavily either on objective or subjective information in the situation imposed by the card sort test. Teachers with advanced training and degrees tend to have somewhat higher scores, indicating more reliance on test scores, but the relationship is not particularly strong.

Teachers who have taken several courses in tests and measurements obtain slightly higher scores on the card sort test, but this relationship does not appear to be strictly a function of the number of courses taken. Even more striking is the lack of significant relationship between card sort scores and reported experience administering and scoring tests or scores on the index of familiarity with tests, two variables which did show significant relationships to the other use items reported in preceding sections of this chapter.

With respect to opinions about the accuracy of tests and their use, only one item, the teacher's belief about the accuracy of standardized tests as a measure of an individual's intellectual potential, is related to greater reliance on objective information on the card sort test (Table 62). The test weight indices described earlier show some relationship to higher card sort scores but nowhere near what might have been expected if one were to assume that opinion and practice were very closely related.[8] This again under-

---

[8] See Goslin, David A., "The Social Impact of Testing in Guidance," *Personnel and Guidance Journal,* vol. 45, March, 1967, pp. 676–682.

Table 62: Public secondary school teachers' opinions about the accuracy of intelligence tests, by card sort test score (Percentages)

CARD SORT TEST SCORE	MUCH BETTER THAN OTHER MEASURES	SLIGHTLY BETTER	NO BETTER	NOT AS GOOD	MUCH WORSE
24 to 29	3.2	3.0	3.3	.0	.0
30 to 39	10.1	13.3	12.5	18.3	.0
40 to 49	14.2	18.8	24.2	26.7	50.0
50 to 59	25.8	26.5	26.0	36.7	40.0
60 to 69	28.1	24.8	22.7	11.7	10.0
70 to 79	15.1	11.2	9.5	3.3	.0
80 to 88	3.5	2.4	1.8	3.3	.0
Number of teachers	(345)	(626)	(273)	(60)	(10)

scores our earlier observations concerning the danger of assuming that there is anything more than a marginal relationship between opinion and practice. We shall consider the implications of this finding in Chapter 7.

Opinions about providing students and their parents with information about test scores are not significantly related to scores on the card sort test, although it will be remembered that many other items associated with a general belief in the efficacy and accuracy of tests did show a relationship to the reporting items.[9] However, teachers who feel that they have a responsibility to prepare pupils for taking standardized tests tend to have higher scores on the card sort. Finally, a tendency to rely more on objective information about pupils is weakly associated with a belief that the abilities measured by standardized tests are more innate than learned, although the relationship is by no means clear-cut (Table 63).

The conclusion that may be drawn from these data is that the card sort test measures something a bit different from either the opinion items or the items concerned with self reports of test use. The consistency of intercorrelations among the various opinions and background items is clearly less pronounced in the case of their relationship to card sort scores than among themselves or in relation to reported use items. This fact leads one to suspect both that the

[9] See pp. 89–97.

Table 63: Public secondary school teachers' opinions about whether the kind of intelligence necessary to do well on standardized intelligence tests is inborn or learned, by card sort test score (Percentages)

CARD SORT TEST SCORE	ONLY INBORN	MORE INBORN THAN LEARNED	EQUALLY INBORN AND LEARNED	MORE LEARNED THAN INBORN	ONLY LEARNED	NO OPINION
24 to 29	6.7	2.4	6.2	5.4	7.3	12.5
30 to 39	6.7	10.7	9.3	14.0	18.2	17.3
40 to 49	20.0	19.3	16.7	20.1	25.2	15.4
50 to 59	20.0	28.1	26.6	26.5	18.2	28.8
60 to 69	26.7	23.1	25.8	23.6	14.5	15.4
70 to 79	20.0	12.9	12.6	8.6	10.9	8.7
80 to 88	.0	2.5	3.8	1.8	5.5	1.9
Number of teachers	(15)	(363)	(365)	(513)	(55)	(104)
Mean Score	(51.3)	(50.0)	(50.8)	(47.8)	(45.8)	(44.1)

opinions and self-report data are subject to some degree of halo effect, and that the card sort may be measuring a deeper level of teacher reliance on test scores than the other items. One implication of this point of view is that more efforts must be made to set up situations by specific tests of teacher reliance on test scores if one is to arrive at firm conclusions about teacher uses of tests.

Card sort scores vs. school and
testing program characteristics

Further evidence of the particular nature of the card sort test is provided by the fact that none of the school characteristics variables, for example, size, type of residential area, percentage of college-bound pupils, or policies concerned with grading and grouping, relate significantly to card sort scores of teachers in the schools. On the other hand, a number of the test use items show a significant correlation with teacher card sort scores.

Consistently higher card sort scores are made by teachers in schools which report that standardized tests are used for: (1) informing pupils of their strengths and weaknesses, (2) counseling parents about the progress of their children, (3) identifying over- and underachievers, (4) informing teachers about their pupils' abilities, (5) grading pupils, and (6) informing pupils about their abilities. Further, we find a positive correlation between teacher reliance on objective measures (as indicated by high card sort scores) and our overall index of extent of test *use* (Table 64) but, interestingly,

Table 64: Index of extent of test use by public secondary school teachers'
card sort test score (Percentages)

CARD SORT TEST SCORE (IN QUARTILES)	EXTENT OF TEST USE (QUARTILES)			
	LITTLE USE			MUCH USE
Low Reliance on Tests	32.4	25.6	24.4	22.8
	27.8	24.8	26.1	23.4
	22.2	24.8	23.9	26.1
High Reliance on Tests	17.6	24.8	25.6	27.7
Number of teachers	(176)	(351)	(360)	(517)

$\chi^2 = 9.26$; $p < .01$ (See Note to Table 24.)

Table 65: Index of extent of testing by public secondary school teachers' card sort test score (Percentages)

CARD SORT TEST SCORE (IN QUARTILES)	EXTENT OF TESTING (QUARTILES)			
	LITTLE TESTING			MUCH TESTING
Low Reliance on Tests	23.4	28.9	20.9	25.6
	24.1	23.8	25.9	26.6
	24.8	24.6	25.6	24.2
High Reliance on Tests	27.7	22.7	27.6	23.5
Number of teachers	(282)	(484)	(340)	(289)

$\chi^2 = .042$; $p < .90$ (See Note to Table 24.)

no correlation between card sort scores and extent of test *giving* (Table 65). In schools where tests are not only given, therefore, but also heavily relied on (at least according to principals' or guidance counselors' reports), teachers also tend to make greater use of test data in filling out the card sort test. This finding lends credence both to the accuracy of the Testing Program Questionnaire and to the validity of the card sort data themselves.

These data imply that a major factor in the extent to which individual teachers rely on standardized test scores is the general school policy regarding tests and their usefulness for various purposes. Such a hypothesis, while by no means directly confirmed by our data, does make it easier to explain inconsistencies in relationships between background characteristics of teachers and their reported use of tests, as well as the lack of correlation between card sort scores and teacher opinions and background.

6

The teacher as a
coach for tests

ONE OF the most frequently voiced criticisms of standardized testing is that it results in excessive efforts on the part of teachers to prepare their students for tests, especially those given in connection with some external testing programs like the College Entrance Examination Board or the New York State Regents' Examinations. The result, it is often claimed, is that teachers emphasize only those things covered by the test to the detriment of other important aspects of their subjects or, even more important, are afraid to introduce innovations in teaching techniques that might result in their students doing poorly on standardized tests. The data presented in this chapter were gathered in an effort to shed some light on the extent to which teachers do, in fact, modify their courses or their methods in an effort to prepare their pupils for standardized tests. Before turning to the findings, however, several preliminary comments are in order.

First, as in the case of the effects of testing examined in preceding sections of this book, the fact that the data are confined to self-reports makes a definitive conclusion about test influence impossible. Once again, the direct evaluation of effects presents a research problem that is exceptionally difficult to overcome without large-

107

scale experimental manipulations, a procedure we were not prepared to undertake without first obtaining the kinds of preliminary observations recorded here.

Second, it is clear that not all standardized tests or testing programs exert the same kinds of potential pressure on teachers to prepare their pupils for the tests. Testing programs sponsored by the school, for example, may not be perceived by the teacher, the pupil, or the pupil's parents as being as important as those given by an external agency such as the College Entrance Examination Board. Unless the teacher feels either that his effectiveness is being evaluated as a consequence of his pupils' performance[1] on the test or that the future opportunities of his students are at stake, it is unlikely that he will feel any pressure to take any action designed to facilitate their performance.

Finally, it should be clear that no value judgment may be made *a priori* about the desirability of a test having an impact on the content of a particular course or curriculum. Presumably, in many cases standardized tests have a beneficial impact on some courses in which teachers make an effort to prepare their students explicitly for the tests. Under many conditions tests may, in fact, have the effect of encouraging innovation on the part of teachers. Thus merely to demonstrate that a significant number of teachers make an effort to prepare pupils for such tests does not necessarily lead to the conclusion that tests are bad. Conversely, demonstration that tests have no such effect may indicate a lack of responsiveness on the part of teachers to developments in their field.

The data presented in this chapter are concerned with: (1) the opinions of teachers about their responsibility to prepare students for standardized tests; (2) teachers' reports of the extent to which they actually have made special efforts to prepare pupils for standardized tests, including whether they have altered either the content of their courses, or teaching methods, as a consequence of knowledge about the content of tests in their field; (3) students' reports of the extent to which any of their teachers have made special efforts to prepare them for standardized tests; (4) reports of teachers on the frequency with which they have received requests from pupils, parents, or other school personnel to prepare students for such tests;

[1] See Chapter 2, p. 23 and Chapter 4, pp. 70–71.

Table 66: Responses of secondary and elementary school teachers and public secondary school counselors to the question, "Do you feel that teachers have a responsibility to try to prepare their students specifically for standardized aptitude or intelligence tests?" (Percentages)

OPINION	SECONDARY SCHOOL TEACHERS			SECONDARY SCHOOL COUNSELORS	ELEMENTARY SCHOOL TEACHERS
	PUBLIC	PRIVATE	PAROCHIAL		
This is a major responsibility	4.6	4.6	6.2	2.8	2.3
This is a minor responsibility	15.8	27.5	23.4	9.2	6.9
Only in some cases	13.5	11.1	15.9	6.4	6.9
No	55.3	52.3	49.7	78.7	75.9
Have no opinion	10.8	4.6	4.8	2.8	8.0
Number of respondents	(1423)	(153)	(145)	(141)	(87)

and (5) the extent to which teachers make use of objective as opposed to essay questions in tests they make up for their pupils.

Teacher opinions about their
responsibility to prepare pupils
for standardized tests

Very few of the teachers in our sample thought that preparing pupils specifically for standardized aptitude, intelligence, or achievement tests is a major responsibility of a teacher. Secondary school teachers were somewhat more inclined to admit that teachers occasionally had such a responsibility than the elementary teachers surveyed, while secondary school counselors in general felt strongly that this was not a responsibility of teachers. (See Tables 66 and 67.) It is interesting to note that a higher proportion of private secondary school teachers tended to feel that preparing students was part of the responsibility of a teacher.

However, when elementary and secondary school teachers were asked whether they would alter their courses in any way if they were to discover that a standardized test used for college admission (at the secondary school level) or ability grouping (at the elementary level) differed significantly in its emphasis from the present content

Table 67: Responses of secondary and elementary school teachers and public secondary school counselors to the question, "Do you feel that teachers have a responsibility to try to prepare their students specifically for standardized achievement tests?" (Percentages)

	SECONDARY SCHOOL TEACHERS			SECONDARY SCHOOL	ELEMENTARY SCHOOL
OPINION	PUBLIC	PRIVATE	PAROCHIAL	COUNSELORS	TEACHERS
This is a major responsibility	3.7	9.2	6.2	2.8	6.8
This is a minor responsibility	17.2	28.1	24.3	9.2	14.8
Only in some cases	12.1	10.5	14.6	3.5	5.7
No	56.1	46.4	49.3	81.0	67.0
Have no opinion	11.0	5.9	5.6	3.5	5.7
Number of respondents	(1424)	(153)	(144)	(142)	(88)

of their course, a majority of the public secondary school teachers expressed the opinion that they would probably or definitely change their course to conform with the test (Table 68). Thus, while teachers apparently are unwilling to acknowledge a view that *specific* preparation of pupils for standardized tests is a part of their role, they do admit that the content of a standardized test would be likely

Table 68: Responses of secondary and elementary school teachers to the question, "If you were to discover that a standardized achievement test which is used for college admission differed in its emphasis on your field from the present content of your course in this subject, do you feel you would change your course in any way?" (Percentages)

	SECONDARY SCHOOL TEACHERS			ELEMENTARY SCHOOL[a]
OPINION	PUBLIC	PRIVATE	PAROCHIAL	TEACHERS
Definitely	10.9	16.2	14.6	7.9
Probably	44.9	31.8	51.4	38.6
Probably not	19.4	25.3	16.0	31.8
Definitely not	4.7	10.4	4.9	3.4
Don't know	20.1	16.2	13.2	18.2
Number of teachers	(1414)	(154)	(144)	(88)

[a] Question 122 on the Elementary Teachers' Questionnaire reads: "If you were to discover that a standardized achievement test which is used to evaluate pupils for grouping (sectioning) in junior high school differed in its emphasis on some subjects from the way you teach your classes, do you feel that you would change your instruction in any way (assuming you were free to do so)?"

Table 69: Opinions of public secondary school teachers of teachers' responsibility to prepare students specifically for standardized tests, by familiarity with tests (Percentages)

	FAMILIARITY WITH TESTS			
OPINION	LITTLE FAMILIARITY		MUCH FAMILIARITY	
This is a major responsibility	3.7	1.9	4.2	4.4
This is a minor responsibility	12.8	17.0	16.7	20.9
Only in some cases	13.5	10.8	15.5	9.9
No	53.4	57.9	55.7	57.1
Have no opinion	16.6	12.4	8.0	7.7
Number of teachers	(295)	(323)	(336)	(364)

$\chi^2 = 2.74$; $p < .20$ (In calculating χ^2, "No opinion" category was eliminated. See also Note to Table 24.)

to have an effect on what or how they teach if the test was significantly different from their current practice.

With respect to teacher background characteristics associated with a belief that it is part of a teacher's responsibility to prepare pupils for tests, we find that only those variables relating to the teacher's familiarity with tests, his opinions about the accuracy of tests, and the weight that should be given to scores in making decisions about pupils are significantly related to the opinions that teachers should specifically prepare pupils for tests. (See Tables 69 to 71.) Other characteristics such as age, sex, amount of education, and major field are not significantly related to opinions in this area. As might be expected, teachers in suburban and urban schools are more likely to feel that this is a part of their job and, interestingly, in schools in which the principal reports that tests are used for grouping pupils according to their abilities, teachers are slightly more likely to feel that preparing students for such tests is at least a minor responsibility.

Teacher reports of the extent to
which they attempt to prepare
pupils for tests

A number of questions were asked of teachers in an effort to get a fairly precise estimate of how much specific preparation of students for standardized tests takes place. These questions covered coaching

Table 70: Opinions of public secondary school teachers of teachers' responsibility to prepare students specifically for standardized tests, by opinion on the accuracy of intelligence or aptitude tests in measuring a student's potential (Percentages)

	OPINION ON ACCURACY					
OPINION	MUCH BETTER THAN OTHER MEASURES	SLIGHTLY BETTER	NO BETTER	NOT AS GOOD	MUCH WORSE	NO OPINION
This is a major responsibility	4.6	3.1	3.5	1.7	.0	5.9
This is a minor responsibility	19.1	19.0	14.5	11.7	.0	10.6
Only in some cases	10.3	14.6	11.7	10.0	11.1	7.1
No	54.1	54.0	61.3	66.7	77.8	47.1
Have no opinion	12.0	9.3	8.9	10.0	11.1	29.4
Number of teachers	(351)	(637)	(282)	(60)	(9)	(85)

$\chi^2 = 7.951$; $p < .01$ (In calculating χ^2, "No opinion" category was eliminated. See also Note to Table 24.)

Table 71: Opinions of public secondary school teachers of teachers' responsibility to prepare students specifically for standardized tests, by total test weight (Percentages)

	TOTAL TEST WEIGHT[a]			
OPINION	LOW WEIGHT			HIGH WEIGHT
This is a major responsibility	2.6	2.2	3.7	5.3
This is a minor responsibility	12.3	18.3	21.0	15.9
Only in some cases	12.6	10.0	12.5	15.0
No	65.2	59.0	52.6	48.4
Have no opinion	7.4	10.5	10.2	15.3
Number of teachers	(310)	(371)	(352)	(339)

$\chi^2 = 14.42$; $p < .001$ (In calculating χ^2, "No opinion" category was eliminated. See also Note to Table 24.)
[a] See Chapter 4, pp. 63–66, for an explanation of the weight indices.

Table 72: Public, private, and parochial secondary school teachers who say
"yes" to three questions about preparing pupils for standardized tests
(Percentages)

| | SECONDARY SCHOOL TEACHERS | | |
PRACTICE	PUBLIC	PRIVATE	PAROCHIAL
Have you ever prepared students for a standardized test by teaching them shortly in advance of the test administration specific information you knew was included in the test?	4.6	3.8	3.4
Number of teachers	(1421)	(156)	(140)
Have you ever prepared students for a standardized test by teaching them shortly in advance of the test administration how to take such tests (how to distribute their time wisely, whether to mark answers to all questions, etc.)?	40.2	51.3	64.8
Number of teachers	(1424)	(156)	(145)
Have you ever prepared students for a standardized test by emphasizing over a considerable period of time the kind of subject matter covered by the test (without any knowledge about specific test items)?	23.9	42.2	34.7
Number of teachers	(1418)	(154)	(144)

of individual students as well as class groups, subject-matter preparation as well as help on techniques for taking tests, and preparation
for intelligence and aptitude tests as well as standardized achievement tests.

Table 72 shows the percentages of public, private, and parochial
secondary school teachers who indicate that they have in the past
prepared students for standardized tests by: (1) teaching them
specific information shortly before the test, (2) teaching them
shortly before the tests how to take such tests, and (3) emphasizing
over a considerable period of time the kind of subject matter covered by the test. Less than 5 per cent of all teachers reported ever
having provided students with specific information they knew would
be on the test shortly in advance of the test administration. While
this is a small percentage, it is interesting that the figure is as high
as it is, since it raises questions about the nature of the students who
receive such special coaching and its impact on their test scores.
With respect to the other two questions, teacher responses support
the contention that a substantial amount of general concern on the

part of teachers with the performance of their students on standardized tests exists, although the answers come as no surprise, considering the previously documented degree of involvement of teachers in the testing process.

Some evidence of specific attempts on the part of teachers to prepare either their classes or individual pupils specifically for standardized tests is provided by responses to other questionnaire items, although very few teachers indicated that this activity was a regular part of their course work. Teachers were asked to what extent they had ever made a "conscious effort to improve their pupils' performance" on different types of standardized tests and under varying circumstances, "either through emphasizing subject matter that they thought might be covered on the test or by giving instruction in how to take tests or answer specific types of questions."[2] Nearly 20 per cent of both elementary and public secondary school teachers surveyed reported that they at least occasionally make efforts to prepare their classes specifically (as defined above) for taking standardized achievement tests. Only a few of the more than fourteen hundred public secondary school teachers reported that this is a major part of a course they teach. Eighty per cent of the public secondary school teachers, 64 per cent of the elementary teachers, 71 per cent of the parochial school teachers, and 56.1 per cent of the private secondary

Table 73: Responses of secondary and elementary school teachers to the question, "Has your knowledge of the content of one or more standardized achievement tests in your field ever caused you to alter the content of the courses taught by you?" (Percentages)

| | SECONDARY SCHOOL TEACHERS | | | ELEMENTARY SCHOOL[a] |
ALTERED CONTENT	PUBLIC	PRIVATE	PAROCHIAL	TEACHERS
On several occasions	3.7	7.1	4.3	5.7
On a few occasions	9.2	14.2	16.3	19.5
Once or twice	2.5	4.5	2.1	12.6
No	66.4	57.4	58.9	48.3
Have no knowledge of the content	14.0	14.2	14.9	6.9
Don't know	4.2	2.6	3.5	6.9
Number of teachers	(1412)	(155)	(141)	(87)

[a] Question 120 on the Elementary Teachers' Questionnaire reads: "Has the knowledge of the content of one or more standardized achievement tests affected the kinds of things you teach in your class?"
[2] See Teachers' Questionnaire, Appendix II.

Table 74: Responses of secondary and elementary school teachers to the question, "Has your knowledge of the content of one or more standardized achievement tests in your field ever caused you to change your teaching methods (but not the content of your courses)?" (Percentages)

CHANGED TEACHING METHODS	SECONDARY SCHOOL TEACHERS			ELEMENTARY SCHOOL TEACHERS
	PUBLIC	PRIVATE	PAROCHIAL	
On several occasions	3.3	4.5	7.0	6.9
On a few occasions	7.9	8.4	9.1	10.3
Once or twice	6.9	7.1	3.5	14.9
No	63.0	65.2	59.4	55.2
Have no knowledge of the content	13.4	12.9	16.1	5.7
Don't know	5.5	1.9	4.9	6.9
Number of teachers	(1410)	(155)	(143)	(87)

school teachers replied that they had never done this. Somewhat smaller proportions of teachers in all groups reported that they had at least occasionally made efforts to prepare their classes specifically for standardized aptitude or intelligence tests.

These figures are in general confirmed by the responses of teachers to questions on whether they have ever changed the content of their courses or their teaching methods as a consequence of knowledge about standardized tests in their field. Tables 73 and 74 summarize these results.

General psychometric sophistication and familiarity with tests that we noted as being related to opinions about tests and test usage in earlier chapters also appear to be related to coaching practices of teachers. The indices of familiarity with tests and experience administering and scoring tests bear a positive relationship to all of the pupil preparation items with the exception of providing pupils with specific information shortly in advance of the administration of the test. (See, for example, Tables 75A and B and 76A and B.) Teachers who think that tests are on the whole accurate measures of a pupil's ability are somewhat more likely to report having made efforts to prepare their students for tests as are those teachers who get high scores on the various test weight indices, although these relationships are not consistent and significant across all of the coaching items. Other background and opinion items that appear to be related to coaching practices include the following: age (older teachers are more likely to coach pupils), opinion that tests are a good

Table 75A: Public secondary school teachers' reports of having prepared students for standardized tests by teaching them how to take tests, by familiarity with tests (Percentages)

	FAMILIARITY WITH TESTS			
PRACTICE	LITTLE FAMILIARITY			MUCH FAMILIARITY
Have prepared students	29.7	32.4	41.2	52.5
Never	70.3	67.6	58.8	47.5
Number of teachers	(296)	(324)	(337)	(362)

$x^2 = 42.00$; $p < .001$ (See Note to Table 24.)

way to evaluate teacher performance, and opinions about the dissemination of test information to pupils and parents.

It should be noted once again that a major factor in the reported tendency of teachers to try to prepare pupils for tests is the teacher's knowledge of the content of standardized tests. Thus most of the items that bear a positive relationship to teacher knowledge about tests also are likely to be related to coaching practices. Consequently, without explicit controls over the variable of familiarity with tests, it is difficult to make very many inferences about the factors that result in coaching activities on the part of teachers. The relatively small amount of coaching reported by teachers, combined with the limited size of the teacher sample, make such controls impractical in the present study. An additional factor that we would expect to be related to attempts on the part of teachers to prepare pupils for tests is the frequency with which they receive requests from their

Table 75B: Public secondary school teachers' reports of having prepared students for standardized tests by teaching them how to take tests, by experience in administering and scoring tests (Percentages)

	EXPERIENCE IN ADMINISTERING AND SCORING TESTS			
PRACTICE	LITTLE EXPERIENCE			MUCH EXPERIENCE
Have prepared students	27.3	42.1	46.2	56.3
Never	72.7	57.9	53.8	43.7
Number of teachers	(586)	(266)	(238)	(341)

$x^2 = 78.94$; $p < .001$

Table 76A: *Public secondary school teachers' reports of having changed their teaching methods because of knowledge of the content of standardized achievement tests, by familiarity with tests (Percentages)*

	FAMILIARITY WITH TESTS			
CHANGED METHODS	LITTLE FAMILIARITY			MUCH FAMILIARITY
On several occasions	2.7	1.6	3.9	3.9
On a few occasions	4.8	8.1	8.3	10.6
Once or twice	3.7	6.3	6.2	11.2
No	63.3	62.2	65.5	61.2
Have no knowledge of the content	18.7	16.9	11.6	6.7
Don't know	6.8	5.0	4.5	6.4
Number of teachers	(294)	(320)	(336)	(358)

$\chi^2 = 10.522; p < .01$ (In calculating χ^2, "No knowledge" and "Don't know" categories were eliminated. See also Note to Table 24.)

pupils or parents of pupils to coach students for tests. Teacher reports of such requests and comparisons between frequency of requests and coaching practices are examined in a later section of this chapter.

Teachers in schools that do a great deal of testing are somewhat

Table 76B: *Public secondary school teachers' reports of having changed their teaching methods because of knowledge of the content of standardized achievement tests, by experience in administering and scoring tests (Percentages)*

	EXPERIENCE IN ADMINISTERING AND SCORING TESTS			
CHANGED METHODS	LITTLE EXPERIENCE			MUCH EXPERIENCE
On several occasions	3.6	2.3	3.4	3.2
On a few occasions	6.0	8.3	5.5	12.6
Once or twice	5.5	6.4	8.5	8.2
No	63.2	64.0	66.9	59.2
Have no knowledge of the content	16.2	15.2	10.6	9.1
Don't know	5.4	3.8	5.1	7.6
Number of teachers	(579)	(264)	(236)	(341)

$\chi^2 = 4.705; p < .05$ (In calculating χ^2, "No knowledge" and "Don't know" categories were eliminated. See also Note to Table 24.)

Table 77: Public secondary school teachers' reports of having prepared students for standardized tests by teaching them how to take tests, by index of extent of testing (Percentages)

	INDEX OF EXTENT OF TESTING			
PRACTICE	LOW TESTING			HIGH TESTING
Have prepared students	32.4	41.6	41.2	44.1
Never	67.5	58.4	58.8	55.9
Number of teachers	(289)	(495)	(345)	(295)

$x^2 = 6.442$; $p < .02$ (See also Note to Table 24.)

more likely to report that they make efforts to prepare pupils for tests (Table 77). Coaching practices also appear to be more prevalent where test information is reported to parents and where tests are used to section pupils according to their abilities (Tables 78 and 79). There is also some evidence that teachers make more effort to coach pupils for tests in schools having a higher proportion of Negroes and a higher dropout rate. The latter findings support the view that there is some sensitivity on the part of teachers to the difficulties cultural deprivation may create for pupils when they face standardized tests. This finding, however, is contradicted by student data reported in the following section.

The rumored extensive existence in public secondary schools of special coaching classes is not supported by our data although a very small number of the teachers in our sample reported having conducted such a class at least once or twice. Ninety-seven per cent

Table 78: Public secondary school teachers' reports of having prepared students for standardized tests, by school policy on giving parents information on pupils' aptitudes for learning school subjects (Percentages)

	SCHOOL POLICY				
PRACTICE	NEVER	PARENT REQUEST	SCHOOL INITIATIVE	ROUTINE	OTHER
Have prepared students	41.2	39.1	34.7	50.0	45.0
Never	58.8	60.9	65.3	50.0	55.0
Number of teachers	(17)	(437)	(525)	(178)	(269)

$x^2 = 17.420$; $p < .001$ (See also Note to Table 24.)

Table 79: Public secondary school teachers' reports of having prepared students for standardized tests, by school policy on importance of tests to section pupils in any given grades by level of mental ability (Percentages)

PRACTICE	SCHOOL POLICY			
	NOT IMPORTANT			VERY IMPORTANT
Have prepared students	33.1	38.3	44.2	46.7
Never	66.9	61.7	55.8	53.3
Number of teachers	(251)	(549)	(543)	(90)

$\chi^2 = 11.10; p < .001$

of the public secondary school teachers indicated they had never taught such a course, while only five of the more than fourteen hundred teachers in these schools said they taught such a course frequently. A somewhat larger proportion of private and parochial school teachers reported having taught such a special class, a finding which, in the case of the private school sample, is clearly the result of a higher proportion of college-preparatory pupils. In the case of the parochial schools, it is probably due to the fact that these are more likely to be urban schools. While the figures are not large at all, the fact that *any* teachers reported having engaged in such activities is interesting since it is unlikely that a particular school would have more than one or two teachers assigned to such a task. Since there were only 75 public secondary schools in the sample, the figure of 42 teachers who said "yes" to this question is of some significance (in addition, 5.1 per cent of the teachers did not respond to this item, a somewhat higher porportion than on most of the other items in the questionnaire).

Student reports of the extent to
which teachers have attempted
to prepare them for tests

Approximately one-fifth of the students who answered the Students' Questionnaire reported that they had taken one or more college entrance or scholarship tests. These students then answered a number of questions about the test(s) they took, including five items concerned directly with the extent to which they had received special preparation or tutoring for the tests. Eighty-one per cent of the 1,170 public school students who reported having taken a college-admissions test indicated that their teachers had spent class time preparing them specifically for the test on at least one or two occasions. Fifty-five per cent of these pupils reported that this had occurred frequently. Thirty per cent replied that on one or more occasions they had spent class time discussing actual copies of standardized tests.

Although this is a select group of students (those who had taken a college-admissions test), the responses to these questions indicate clearly that the majority of pupils who are headed for a college requiring entrance tests receive some special preparation for the tests they will have to take. In addition to the obvious impact on the kinds of things that are taught in school, these findings raise some interesting questions concerning the effects of inequities in the amount of special assistance and preparation provided for different groups of pupils. What is the effect, for example, of not having received any such assistance on the test scores achieved and on the consequent admission chances of those pupils who do not receive assistance? Studies sponsored by the College Entrance Examination Board of the effect of coaching indicate that coaching has little effect on scores. But the fact that so many pupils have received some kind of special preparation in school raises the possibility that the studies made by the College Board may be contaminated by informal activities of teachers prior to the research. Our data thus indicate the need for further research on the effects of coaching in situations where *no prior* special preparation has been given.

Comparisons between the coaching items on the Students' Questionnaire and school characteristics as reported on the Testing Program Questionnaire confirm the expectation that more special preparation for standardized tests goes on in schools having a high proportion of college-bound pupils, urban and suburban schools, schools in middle- and upper-income areas, schools that have extensive testing programs of their own, and schools in which the principal reports that scores are reported to parents. Recalling that only students who had taken a college-entrance test were asked to respond to the coaching item on the Students' Questionnaire, it is apparent that college-bound pupils in predominantly college-preparatory secondary schools are likely to receive more preparation for college-entrance tests than similar students in schools having a small proportion of college-preparatory students. This fact suggests that secondary schools with a small proportion of college-bound students have a particular responsibility to make special arrangements to help prepare these pupils to take entrance examinations if they are to have a chance to compete on an equal basis with pupils coming from college-preparatory schools.

Teacher reports of requests to prepare
pupils for standardized tests

It was hypothesized that an important factor in the decision of a teacher to attempt to prepare his students specifically for standardized tests would be requests from school administrators, guidance personnel, parents, or pupils themselves, to provide such special preparation. Consequently, teachers were asked a series of questions concerning the extent of such requests from each of the parties mentioned above.

The overwhelming conclusion that may be drawn from our data is that except for occasional requests from pupils, teachers almost never are asked to provide special preparation for standardized tests. Only sixteen of the more than fourteen hundred public secondary school teachers reported ever having been asked by a guidance counselor to alter the content of one of their courses for this purpose. Twenty teachers reported having been asked by a guidance counselor to change their teaching methods on one or more occasions, and another (or the same) twenty to conduct special classes designed to prepare pupils for tests. Comparable numbers reported requests from their principal or from parents to alter content or method of courses they teach. About 5 per cent of the public secondary school teachers (72 out of 1,450) reported that their pupils had requested such assistance on at least one occasion (Table 80). Only two or three of the elementary teachers in our sample indicated that they had ever received a request of this nature from either the school principal or from parents.

Although comparisons between request items and reports by teachers that they have made attempts to prepare pupils for tests are positively correlated, it is clear from these findings that requests of this nature are not the major factor in a teacher's decision to alter

Table 80: Responses of public, private, and parochial secondary school teachers to the question, "Have you ever been asked by any of your pupils to alter the content of any of your courses so that they would be better prepared for standardized tests?" (Percentages)

	SECONDARY SCHOOL TEACHERS		
ASKED TO ALTER CONTENT	PUBLIC	PRIVATE	PAROCHIAL
On several occasions	.4	.0	1.4
On a few occasions	1.5	4.5	2.1
On one or two occasions	3.2	8.4	6.3
No	94.1	85.7	89.4
Don't know or can't remember	.9	1.2	.7
Number of teachers	(1423)	(154)	(142)

his course or his teaching methods, or to instruct pupils specifically in test-taking techniques. Further research is indicated on the role general school policy or other system pressures play in this process, as well as on the kinds of orientation teacher-education programs are currently giving teachers toward tests and their responsibility to prepare pupils to take them.

Teacher uses of objective vs.
essay tests

A final way in which teachers may help to prepare pupils for standardized tests is through the use of objective tests of their own in courses they teach. It seems likely that the increased use of objective tests in education, not only for guidance and college entrance, but also for systematic pupil evaluation at all stages has caused teachers to make greater use of objective tests of their own in evaluating pupils progress in their classes. Only 7 per cent of the public secondary school teachers and only 2 per cent of the elementary teachers surveyed reported that they never use objective (multiple-choice, true-false, matching, or completion) questions in tests that they prepare for their students (Table 81). Conversely, 67 per cent of the public secondary school teachers and 76 per cent of the elementary teachers report using objective items frequently, most of the time, or always. Although no comparative data exist to make possible estimates of the extent to which these figures represent increases on the part of teachers in the use of objective measurement techniques, it is hardly conceivable that such a result would have been obtained thirty, or even twenty, years ago.

Further support for the contention that there has been an increase in the use of objective questions in teacher-made tests is provided by the sharp contrast between public and private school teachers on this item. Forty-two per cent of the private school teachers reported that they never use objective items on tests they prepare for their pupils and only about 13 per cent use such items frequently. This finding may be due in part to differences in the size of classes in public as opposed to private schools. Our data also indicate that younger teachers are more likely than older teachers to use objective items, as are male teachers as opposed to female teachers. While part of the private-public difference may be due to a greater emphasis in private schools on the humanities (where objective tests construction is more difficult), and the difference between men and women teachers is probably due in part to the fact that more men teach science or mathematics (where objective tests may be more useful), it does not seem likely that the discrepancy can be explained wholly in these terms. If we assume that private education is more likely to be traditionally oriented and the public schools more susceptible to such factors as the increase in student enrollments which necessitate the development of procedures for dealing with larger groups of

Table 81: Responses of public, private, and parochial secondary school teachers and elementary school teachers to the question, "How frequently do you use objective (that is, multiple-choice, true-false, matching, or completion) questions in tests that you prepare for your students?" (Percentages)

	SECONDARY SCHOOL TEACHERS			ELEMENTARY SCHOOL TEACHERS
USE OBJECTIVE QUESTIONS	PUBLIC	PRIVATE	PAROCHIAL	
Always or nearly always	12.3	2.6	13.1	5.7
Most of the time	22.5	.7	20.7	23.9
Frequently	32.7	13.1	38.6	46.6
Occasionally	25.1	41.2	24.1	21.5
Never or almost never	7.4	42.5	3.4	2.3
Number of teachers	(1482)	(153)	(145)	(88)

Table 82: *Responses of public, private, and parochial secondary school teachers, and elementary school teachers to the question, "How frequently do you use essay or short essay questions in tests that you prepare for your students?" (Percentages)*

USE ESSAY QUESTIONS	SECONDARY SCHOOL TEACHERS			ELEMENTARY SCHOOL TEACHERS
	PUBLIC	PRIVATE	PAROCHIAL	
Always or nearly always	7.6	26.5	13.2	1.1
Most of the time	14.9	27.1	13.2	18.2
Frequently	31.8	19.4	41.0	38.6
Occasionally	31.9	13.5	27.8	39.8
Never or almost never	13.9	13.5	4.9	2.3
Number of teachers	(1422)	(155)	(144)	(88)

students simultaneously, these differences are predictable. Nevertheless, they underscore the importance of the impact standardized testing technology has had on a major aspect of the educational process.

It should be noted that the use of objective test items by teachers does not in any way preclude the continued and simultaneous use of essay-type questions by the same teachers. In part our data support this view, although the figures summarized in Table 82 indicate that 31.9 per cent of the public secondary school teachers surveyed use essay-type questions only occasionally in their tests and only 22 per cent use such questions most or all of the time. Although, again, no historical comparative data exist, it would appear that the complaints of colleges that their entrants are not so well versed in writing skills as they used to be may have some basis in fact. This problem is one that deserves much more thorough research, including a detailed survey of the actual frequency with which students are required to write essays as part of tests in different subjects.

With respect to the question of what kinds of teachers tend to use objective as opposed to essay-type questions, several interesting findings result. First, as expected, those teachers who have a high opinion of the accuracy of standardized tests are more likely to make use of objective items on tests they make up for their pupils. But greater familiarity with standardized test instruments and more experience administering and scoring tests do *not* lead to greater employment of objective questions. Third, teachers who favor providing pupils with test information are more likely to use objective items on their tests; and finally, teachers who feel that they have a responsibility to prepare pupils for standardized tests are more likely to give objective type tests. Thus, with the exception of the familiarity and experience with test indices, we find that the "psychometric orientation" on the part of the teacher influences his behavior with respect to an important area of his role as a teacher.

7

Conclusion

In this report we have tried to present as complete and detailed a picture of teacher involvement in standardized testing as survey data permit. Many of the findings must be viewed as tentative owing to the nature of the various samples of respondents from whom data were gathered. As in any survey, many results made us wish that additional or different questions had been asked originally. In a number of cases the findings raised more questions than they answered and the resolution of these issues awaits further investigation.

Public elementary school teachers and students; public, private, and parochial secondary school teachers, students, and officials; public secondary school counselors; and parents of elementary school children responded to a variety of questionnaire items concerning: (1) familiarity with and experience in administering and scoring standardized tests, (2) opinions about the accuracy, fairness, and usefulness of standardized tests, (3) actual uses of tests, including reporting of scores to pupils and parents, and (4) teacher practices with respect to preparing students specifically for taking standardized tests. In this chapter we would like to consider some of the implications of our findings for school policies concerned with testing, for training programs in tests and measurement, and for the testing industry in general.

126

Teacher training in measurement
techniques and theory

With respect to formal training in test and measurement techniques (courses taken in college, attendance at clinics on standardized testing, and the like), our data indicate that less than 40 per cent of all teachers have had more than minimal exposure (one course) to such training, and that a sizable proportion of teachers have never had a course in measurement techniques or attended a clinic at which testing was discussed. Elementary and private secondary school teachers in particular report a lack of exposure to formal instruction in measurement with more than half of those who responded to our questionnaires indicating that they had never had any special training.

At the same time nearly three-fourths of the elementary teachers in our sample reported that they were routinely responsible for administering standardized achievement tests to their pupils each year. Although relatively few secondary teachers have routine testing responsibilities, 49.6 per cent of the public secondary school teachers reported having administered achievement tests at least once since they began teaching and 26.7 per cent had given a group intelligence test. Even more significant is the finding that in virtually all schools teachers have easy access to their pupils' test scores and that in most elementary schools intelligence and achievement scores are routinely distributed to teachers. Less than 10 per cent of the teachers in all groups surveyed indicated that they had never known any pupil's IQ score, and at the elementary level, principals reported that teachers are given test scores more than 80 per cent of the time in all grades.

It may be argued with considerable logic that it is not necessary for an elementary or secondary school teacher to have had a formal course in tests and measurement in order to be able to administer a standardized achievement or intelligence test to a group of pupils. As long as the teacher's responsibility in the testing process is restricted to following a set of printed instructions for administering and scoring a particular standardized test it is difficult to dispute this point. The fact that he possesses his pupils' scores on standardized tests, however, places the teacher in the position of being more than a mere test administrator.

It is, of course, extremely difficult to make inferences, especially from survey data, about the extent to which possession of intelligence or other standardized test scores influence teacher attitudes and behavior toward pupils. One recent study conducted by Robert Rosenthal of Harvard University[1] indicates that teacher expectations concerning pupils' performance may influence actual student behavior markedly. Early in the school year Rosenthal gave elementary school pupils a test which was purportedly designed to identify those pupils who would be likely to show marked gains in intellectual ability during the coming year. Teachers were given the results of the test and told that they could expect substantial IQ gains on the part of those pupils who had done well. Actually, the test was a sham, and high scores were reported for ten children in each class who had been selected randomly to constitute an experimental group, the remainder of the children in each class serving as the control group. At the end of the school year the children were retested and the experimental group in the first, second, and third grades showed an average gain of 25 IQ points over the control group, which, incidentally, also showed some gains. The effect did not appear in the upper three elementary grades, but the startling results obtained in grades one through three point to the strong potential impact of teacher expectations on pupil performance.

The effect of teacher sophistication in the philosophy and practice of pupil measurement was not explicitly tested in the Rosenthal experiment, but from our data it may be assumed that most of the teachers involved in that study were relatively uninformed with respect to the nature and use of standardized tests. Whether increased sophistication would have altered the results (in either direction) is, of course, unknown. What is clear, however, is that we can no longer consider teachers to be innocent bystanders in the evaluation process. To the extent that teachers administer standardized tests to their pupils and are charged with responsibility for scoring these tests or are routinely given access to their pupils' scores, some impact on teacher perceptions of their pupils would seem to be inevitable. And the nature of this impact as well as the effect of the teachers' expectations, in turn, on the pupils involved will very likely be influenced by the way the teachers view the tests.

[1] Rosenthal, Robert, and Lenore Jacobson, *Pygmalion in the Classroom: Self-Fulfilling Prophecies and Teacher Expectations.* Unpublished manuscript.

One conclusion that may be drawn from our research, therefore, is that explicit consideration needs to be given to the problem of teacher training in the field of measurement. What kinds of training ought to be given and the degree of teacher sophistication to be sought may not be specified without further investigation. Elementary teachers would appear to be the group most in need of attention because of their greater initial lack of training, their greater responsibility in the testing process, and the greater susceptibility of their pupils to the influence of teacher expectations. Aside from possible modifications in the curriculum of teacher training institutions to include more formal training in testing, increased sophistication on the part of elementary teachers might be achieved through the publication of a short booklet designed explicitly to deal with the problems faced by elementary teachers in their role as testers. Such a booklet might be prepared under the sponsorship of the American Psychological Association and distributed *en masse* to elementary teachers through the American Council on Education, the National Education Association, or some similar organization. Furthermore, school systems and testing specialists within them might be encouraged to initiate informal training programs or clinics for teachers (and perhaps, ultimately, for parents as well).

One could specify various additional and alternative plans for teaching teachers about tests. Our data indicate that teacher involvement in testing is both high and of potentially great influence on the educational system and the children within it. If we accept testing and the use of test results as a part of the teacher role, efforts need to be made to make sure that this part of their role is not carried out in a context of naïveté about tests and what they measure.

Opinions concerning the nature of
intelligence and accuracy of tests

The questionnaire data presented in Chapter 4 provide an overall picture of teacher attitudes toward and beliefs about standardized tests and the qualities they measure. In its broad outlines, this picture has the following general characteristics: First, teachers tend to view standardized tests as relatively accurate measures of a student's intellectual potential and achievements. Second, teachers see the kinds of abilities measured by standardized tests as important determinants of the subsequent academic success of children, and, to a lesser extent, of their success in life after school. Third, they believe that considerable weight should be given to test scores, along with other measures such as school grades, in making decisions about allocating pupils to special classes, recommending students for college admissions, and the like. Fourth, they tend to view the kind of skills measured by standardized tests, including those designed to evaluate intelligence, as being more influenced by learning than by innate capabilities. In this case public school teachers are more like pupils and parents in their attitudes than they are like guidance counselors and the parochial school teachers, who evidence a more genetic view of the kinds of intelligence measured by tests. At the same time, however, a significant finding of our research is that there is a high degree of disagreement on this point not only among the teachers surveyed, but among guidance counselors and others as well. Finally, with respect to the problem of whether teachers should give pupils information about their (the pupils') performance on standardized tests, particularly intelligence tests, the opinions of teachers are divided, although a clear finding is that nearly all teachers feel some children should be given such information, depending on the circumstances.

With respect to our general theme of attitude consistency, we may conclude that our data provide evidence of a degree of internal consistency in the belief systems of teachers concerning tests and their use. Teachers who express confidence in the accuracy of standardized tests also feel that they measure the qualities necessary for success in future academic and nonacademic pursuits. They also believe that the abilities measured are, to a significant degree, innate, rather than learned. Further, they feel that considerable weight should be given to test scores in making decisions about pupils. Teachers who express all of these opinions tend to have had more contact with tests through having served as test administrators, and more formal training in psychometrics. In general, the more they resemble counselors in their training and experience, the more they express opinions similar to those expressed by counselors. All of this points to the existence in some teachers of a belief system we might label as psychometric sophistication. To the extent that we provide teachers with more and better training in the theory and practice of testing, the more teachers are likely to hold opinions about tests that are consistent and positive.

The overall degree of confidence in tests expressed by teachers supports our contention that the part played by teachers in the testing process is an important one. Teachers not only have ready access to test scores and frequently take part in the administration and scoring of tests; they also tend to view the results of tests as accurately reflecting important qualities of the pupils tested. On the other hand, ambivalence on the part of teachers concerning the nature of intelligence as measured by tests and whether pupils should be given information about their performance on tests is manifested in our data.

Whether a teacher views tested intelligence as being primarily learned or innate is likely to be an important influence on the way that teacher reacts to reports of the performance of his pupils on a standardized test. If the teacher views standardized tests as measuring essentially past learning, there is likely to be less of a tendency for the teacher to put pupils into more or less fixed ability categories or to view some pupils as having strictly limited capacities and others as having abilities that automatically assure them of success. Consequently, we would expect that tests would have less of the self-fulfilling prophecy characteristics demonstrated by Rosenthal in cases where teachers held a predominantly learning-oriented view of the test results.

Leaving for a moment the question of whether or not intelligence or aptitude tests actually measure innate capabilities to any substantial degree, we may conclude that there are likely to be certain advantages for the school system and for pupils in it if teachers are unwilling to accept the presupposition that a pupil's score reflects his inherent (and therefore, presumably, unchangeable) abilities. How one reconciles this proposition with the facts in the situation, namely, that intelligence tests do measure innate abilities to some degree, however, is less clear. It is probably unrealistic to consider seriously attempting systematically to dupe teachers into thinking that tests do not measure innate abilities or that there are no such things as genetically influenced individual differences in capacity for learning. Furthermore, our data strongly imply that as a teacher's or guidance counselor's sophistication in the use of tests increases as a result of training or experience, his opinions are likely to shift in the direction of greater emphasis on innate abilities. Thus, in calling for greater efforts to train teachers in the theory and practice of testing (as we have just done), we are faced with the prospect of accentuating the tendency to classify children according to their (innate) abilities.

One solution that frequently has been proposed in one form or another and that was adopted by the New York City school system is the elimination of instruments labeled as intelligence tests, or, at least, the abandonment of the concept of IQ. While this remedy may serve to promote a learning-oriented conception of intellectual abilities on the part of teachers and other test users, it may create other problems. In attempting to hide the fact that individual differences in learning capacity do exist, such a policy may result in teachers and others using less appropriate measures, for example, reading test scores, to make inferences about the intellectual capacities of children. In communities where a sizable proportion of the school-going population may be expected to have reading difficulties due to deprivation during their early years or the fact that a foreign language is spoken at home, an intelligence test (especially one that emphasizes nonverbal skills) is likely to be a much more useful device for assessing the abilities of pupils, particularly during the first few years of school.

The problem is one of making sure that the measurement process takes into account as many aspects of a child's background and current characteristics as possible and provides him with maximum opportunity to demonstrate his abilities, while at the same time guarding against the tendency toward premature labeling or categorization that results from an overemphasis on test scores coupled with a more or less rigidly genetic view of ability. This depends not only on the ability of teachers to view test scores as probability statements that are subject to variation and that reflect the special circumstances of particular children, but also on the flexibility of the bureaucratic organization within which the testing takes place. The latter problem requires special attention in large school systems that must deal with a great number and variety of pupils in a uniform manner in order to avoid charges of favoritism on the one hand and attempted influence by parents on the other.

The last major finding relating to the opinions of teachers is the high degree of ambivalence about whether teachers should give pupils or their parents test scores. In this respect, teachers reflect the uncertainty that exists generally in the field of measurement in regard to the problem of disseminating test score information. Thus far no clear policy recommendations on this point have been advanced by any individual or group in the field and careful research on the effects of giving children test scores has been minimal at best. School policies consequently vary radically on this issue although most schools refrain from disseminating intelligence test scores routinely to either parents or pupils. A number of interesting issues are raised by these findings. However, since a consideration of teacher practices, as well as opinion, is required in this case, we shall withhold comment until the end of the following section.

Teacher uses of tests

Data were gathered from teachers concerning three specific possible uses of test results: in grading pupils, in advising them about their work in the teacher's course, and in providing pupils and their parents with information about their abilities. In answer to direct questions covering these three aspects of test use, teachers in general indicated a rather low degree of use of test scores. For example, more than three-quarters of our respondents indicated that they had never made use of a pupil's intelligence test score in assigning a grade; a similar proportion reported that they had never or only occasionally used intelligence test scores in advising one of their pupils concerning his work in their course; and over 80 per cent replied that they had never given a student specific information about his intelligence based on a test score.

Despite the rather low overall use of test scores by teachers, our data indicate that in situations where more standardized tests are given by the school, where teachers are routinely given scores, and where greater efforts are made by the school to encourage test score use, greater use is reported by teachers in all cases. In addition, those teachers who have had more training in tests and measurement techniques, more experience administering and scoring tests, and who evidence greater familiarity with tests tend to make greater use of test scores. One conclusion that may be drawn from our data, therefore, is that teacher use of tests depends to some extent on school use of tests, and, furthermore, that increased teacher sophistication in pupil measurement is likely to lead to greater use of test scores in grading, advising students, and the like.

Among other issues, our findings raise the question of the extent to which teachers are, and ought to be, involved in counseling and advising pupils. Traditionally, of course, teachers have always been expected to evaluate their pupils' work and to provide them with advice and guidance concerning their classroom performance. Almost inevitably the provision of such guidance involves judgments on the part of the teachers about a pupil's intellectual capacity in general and his ability to master the specific skills the teacher is responsible for inculcating. Whether or not teachers report that they make conscious use of intelligence and other standardized test results in deciding what to tell their students, it is unlikely that such information, if it reaches the teacher, will not have some influence on the way the teacher responds to his pupils.

As schools and school systems have grown in size, pupil services of all types have become increasingly specialized. In this process the roles of guidance counselor and testing specialist have assumed greater importance and have become more clearly defined in many schools, particularly at the secondary level. As a consequence, teachers are less likely to perceive their own role as including formal counseling of pupils. On the other hand, teachers often feel that they know more about their students than the school counselor or other administrative personnel whose contact with individual pupils is likely to be infrequent at best. Given this situation, we would predict a high degree of ambivalence on the part of teachers with respect to the extent to which they ought to engage in counseling their pupils, a hypothesis which is indirectly borne out by the opinion data presented above, and by data on the relation between opinion and practice.

On the question of whether teachers should provide pupils with information about their abilities based on intelligence test scores, diverse opinions were expressed by the teachers in our sample, as we noted above. Very few teachers felt that all pupils should be given either specific or general information about their intelligence, but most expressed the opinion that such information should be given to at least some pupils. In practice, however, it would appear from our data that very few teachers ever give their students such information. Nearly half of the public high school teachers and 60 per cent of the elementary school teachers reported that they had never given a pupil even a general idea of his intelligence (despite the fact that our data show clearly that nearly all teachers possess intelligence test scores for some if not all of their students). As we have pointed out several times, even among those teachers who expressed the opinion that all pupils should be given information about their abilities, we found a sizable number who had never given a student such information.

Against the backdrop of conflicting and ambivalent school policies and teacher practices concerning the dissemination of intelligence test results, we encountered strong feelings on the part of both students and parents that they would like to have such information and also evidence that a considerable amount of information does find its way into the hands of some students. An intelligence test score or a general interpretation of it may, of course, reach a pupil or his parents through various means. The school principal, guidance counselor, testing specialist, or the teacher may provide the feedback. Many children learn their scores as a result of an illicit look at pupil records left inadvertently on a teacher's desk or entrusted to a student to deliver to the office. But the process remains essentially an unstructured one with the likelihood of a student's finding out his score being dependent upon chance factors, his or his parents' interest and perseverance, and the initiative of teachers or other school officials.

The problems of whether or not students ought to be given test results, including intelligence test scores, and, if so, what role teachers should be expected to play in the counseling process remain unresolved. It does seem clear, however, that school policies on this issue need clarification. As school testing programs and practices become more visible to parents it seems likely that there will be increased interest on their part in finding out about their children's abilities and in knowing on what information the school is basing its decisions to allocate their children to special instructional groups, to admit or not admit them to college preparatory tracks, to offer them remedial services, and the like. From a legal standpoint a strong case can be made (and already has been made on one occasion)[2] for the contention that parents have a right to information such as intelligence test scores possessed by the school about their children.

As long as pupil evaluation is carried out in an atmosphere of semisecrecy and in the absence of clear policies regarding dissemination of the results of the evaluative process, some inequities would appear to be unavoidable. Children whose parents take the time and trouble to inquire about test scores or whose teachers take an interest in them are more likely to receive guidance that may be instrumental in sustaining motivation, or in encouraging them to consider occupational alternatives not previously viewed as realistic. It may be assumed that most schools do make efforts to counsel pupils in those cases where significant discrepancies are noted between ability and performance, or between ability and aspiration level. But a great deal of the initiative still is left to the child and his parents, a problem which becomes particularly acute in overcrowded and understaffed schools that tend to be in areas where parental (and pupil) interest is low.

At this point very little of a systematic nature is known about the effects on children of providing them with specific information about their abilities. Obviously, the effect depends upon the information given, previously held conceptions of ability, the way in which the information is presented, the strength of competing estimates, and various other factors. Some of these variables will be considered is a forthcoming volume by Orville G. Brim, Jr., and others on *American Attitudes Toward Intelligence*.[3] But as long as the likelihood of a given child's receiving information and the manner in which it is presented to him, if he does receive it, are left to chance, we are not in a position either to make sure that harmful effects are avoided or that beneficial effects are uniformly obtained. To the extent that we are committed to standardized testing as a major adjunct to our educational system, we must face up to the problem of developing a rational policy with respect to the dissemination of test results.

[2] In New York State a decision rendered by State Supreme Court Justice William Brennan on January 19, 1961, in a suit brought by a Long Island parent to compel school officials to show him his child's records, upheld the right of the parent to find out his child's test score, provided it was part of the official school record [Van Allen v. McCleary 27 Misc. 2d 81, 211 NYS 2d 501 (Sup. Ct. Nassau Co. 1961)].

[3] To be published by Russell Sage Foundation.

Whether or not the policy that emerges permits us to realize the potential of tests for helping all children to acquire a realistic perception of their capabilities depends on continued research efforts in this area and a willingness on the part of all those involved in the testing industry to consider the sociological as well as the measurement implications of their instruments.

Coaching for tests

Our data indicate that "coaching" for tests has not as yet become a major part of the activity of teachers in our public schools although efforts to prepare pupils more adequately for tests are made by many teachers. There is some evidence, however, that these efforts are not equally distributed among all of the potential recipients, mainly college-bound students in our study. Thus, while it appears that fears of mass coaching are groundless, some attention to the problem of making sure that all pupils who must take standardized tests receive at least minimum preparation is indicated in order that we avoid creating unnecessary barriers for the pupil whose teachers do not at present make such efforts. It may be that such preparation (not mass or intensive coaching) will have to be provided on a more or less systematic basis in our schools in order to reduce the inequities that result from leaving so crucial a matter entirely to teacher initiative.

It is also clear that the use of objective-type items by teachers in their own tests is virtually universal. It may be presumed that much of this test construction is done with, at most, minimal sophistication on the part of the teacher in the methods of objective testing or item writing. If the advantages of objective testing are to be fully realized and its pitfalls avoided, it seems clear that our teacher training institutions will have to pay increased attention to the problems of test construction as they apply to the classroom teacher and provide our future teachers with the kinds of skills they will need to do an adequate job of making tests. This is an area in which testing firms might perform a particularly useful role in helping schools of education to develop practical courses in test construction.

Finally, to return to a point made at the beginning of this chapter, one could argue that our data indicate that tests have failed to fulfill a major part of their function because there is little direct evidence that they have had an impact on teaching methods or course content. The point could be made that such an influence, had it been observed, would have been a sign that our educational institutions in general and teachers in particular were sensitive to the changes occurring in many fields of knowledge that are reflected in tests covering new subject matter or old subjects in new ways. These critics would have hoped for more evidence of adaptability on the part of teachers, and will no doubt be distressed by our results. As we pointed out above, tests can, and should in many instances (for example, the "new" math), serve as stimulants to innovation on the part of teachers. While on the one hand, it is somewhat reassuring to learn that teachers are not blindly teaching children how to take tests, it is just a bit disconcerting to find that so little modification of courses is taking place. This issue is very definitely one on which further work is needed.

Opinions vs. practices

A major theme of this book has been the relationship between opinions and practices. It is apparent from the data presented that in several instances opinions expressed by teachers concerning the proper use of tests diverge from actual practices involving tests. These inconsistencies appear most clearly in comparisons between opinions regarding the amount of weight that should be given test scores and the results of the card sort test, and in comparisons between the opinions of teachers about giving pupils test scores and their reports of whether they had ever done so. (See Chapter 5.)

As we pointed out, the discovery of such inconsistencies is not particularly startling in the light of a succession of studies showing similar findings in other fields (for example, voting behavior). The opinions expressed by an individual are the result of a number of factors, including the beliefs of members of his immediate reference group, his background and training, and his perception of what kinds of answers his interrogator would like to hear. This behavior, however, is the product of various situational determinants of his role, including formal and informal constraints, the presence or absence of pressures to act, and competing demands on his time and energy. Consequently, it would be surprising if we were to find a perfect correlation between opinion and practice.

We have shown that teachers' opinions regarding tests and their use are closely related to their experience and familiarity with tests and to their formal training in psychometrics. Furthermore, we have demonstrated a degree of consistency of belief regarding tests on the part of teachers as well as other groups. On the other hand, we have noted that school policies with respect to such things as reporting test scores to pupils tend to be ill-defined. Formal specification of the teacher role in the area of counseling and guidance is almost non-existent. Even though in most schools teachers are generally encouraged to use test scores to "individualize" their teaching procedures in order to meet the special needs of individual pupils, how they are to do this is left almost entirely to the initiative of the teachers. As a result, except for occasional requests for information from parents, most teachers encounter no specific pressures from those who mainly define their role to make use of test scores in any particular way. Consequently, while a teacher may express various opinions about tests, these opinions may have very little relation to his behavior. This conclusion is borne out in the data presented throughout this book. It remains for us to consider its implications for educational policy regarding standardized testing.

Teachers, testing, and the school

Despite a continuing trend toward specialization in our schools, there is very little doubt that teachers will continue to be heavily involved in standardized testing; partly as a result of their role in test administration, especially in elementary school, but more important, because standardized tests will continue to be used to evaluate the achievements and intellectual potential of their pupils. During the past half-century literally thousands of speeches, papers, and books have been written on the subject of the proper use of information generated by standardized testing programs. A significant proportion of this output has been directed at teacher uses of tests. Yet we find little evidence that it has resulted in the formulation of school policies that clearly specify what teachers are supposed to do with test scores. In playing his role, a teacher responds to the expectations of school administrators, colleagues, parents, and his pupils, as well as to broader societal norms relating to teacher conduct. Where these expectations are clearly defined, transmitted, and sanctioned, he can be expected to incorporate them into the role he plays, assuming that they do not conflict with expectations transmitted by other parts of his role set. Where there is a lack of role definition or role conflict on the other hand, we find ambivalence, inconsistent behavior, or no behavior at all.

It would appear from our data that this describes the situation teachers face with respect to the use of test scores. School policies, as we have noted, are vague and inconsistent, and where they do exist they are likely to conflict with the expectations of parents and pupils, for example, in the case of requests for test scores. We have attempted to provide partial documentation of the resulting ambivalent behavior on the part of teachers.

The solution to this problem would seem to be in clearer specification of all aspects of the teacher's role as it involves standardized testing. This specification must take the form of explicit school policies concerning such things as the dissemination of test scores to pupils and parents, the teacher's more general responsibilities for counseling and guidance, the uses teachers are expected to make of test scores in individualizing instructional practices along with procedures for carrying out this aspect of their duties, and the part to be played by test results in evaluating curricula as well as teacher performance. Major policy decisions are clearly involved here and in several instances additional research is indicated before such decisions can be made intelligently. But a beginning can and should be made now. The role of teachers in testing is too important to be left to chance.

Appendices

APPENDIX I

Sampling and data collection procedures— secondary schools[1]

Selecting the sample

In this study we were concerned with the opinions and attitudes of senior high school students, teachers, and counselors regarding standardized tests of ability. Our primary concern was to obtain data that could be generalized to each of these populations in public senior high schools. A secondary interest was in obtaining samples of private and Roman Catholic parochial schools,[2] to enable us to make certain comparisons with the data from the public school group.

For the public senior high schools the sample was selected in such a way that it would be representative of the respective national populations for the school year 1963–1964. This requirement dictated the use of a sampling procedure designed to achieve representation of public schools on a number of dimensions demonstrated[3]

[1] Excerpted from Brim, Orville G., Jr., David A. Goslin, David C. Glass, and Isadore Goldberg, *The Use of Standardized Ability Tests in American Secondary Schools and Their Impact on Students, Teachers, and Administrators*, Technical Report No. 3 on the Social Consequences of Testing. Russell Sage Foundation, New York, 1965, pp. 17–28.

[2] Roman Catholic schools may be parochial or diocesan, the former associated with the parish and latter with the diocese. The term "parochial" will be used in this report to cover both types of schools.

[3] Flanagan, John C., John T. Dailey, Marion F. Shaycoft, David G. Orr, and Isadore Goldberg, *Studies of the American High School*, Technical Report to the U.S. Office of Education, Cooperative Research Project, No. 226. Project Talent Office, University of Pittsburgh, Pittsburgh, 1962.

to be related to school testing practices and policies and to school-wide averages of students' scores on standardized aptitude and achievement measures. The aim in selecting the private schools and the parochial schools was not at all the same. In these samples the major purpose was to study special groups of students. We wanted a sample of private schools that represented the "elite" senior high school and student. Therefore, the sample was made up of schools which, in the judgment of the staff of Russell Sage Foundation and the University of Pittsburgh were outstanding in academic requirements, reputation, and performance.

It was felt that parochial schools may be sufficiently different to justify their separate treatment. From a statistical standpoint, there are difficulties in drawing representative samples from this group of schools. The procedures used are described later in this report. Suffice it to say that the sample of schools obtained was not drawn by statistical sampling procedures, yet it represents a distribution of parochial schools varying widely in testing policies and practices and in student abilities and beliefs.

It was decided to aim for a sample of 80 public senior high schools, 10 private high schools, and 10 parochial high schools. A senior high school was defined as one which includes grade 10 and grade 12. The public school sample did *not* include schools that offer only the vocational curriculum as Dailey[4] demonstrated that vocational schools in 1960 differed in certain respects from the comprehensive high school and the academically oriented high school.

With regard to the sample of students, it was felt that adequate representation of a cross-section of high school students could be achieved by sampling from grade 10 and grade 12. We decided to aim for a sample of approximately 4,000 students. Information on school enrollments and from Project Talent[5] suggested that considerably more than 4,000 students would likely be obtained if the grade 10 and grade 12 students in all 100 schools participated in the project. Two steps were taken to keep the student sample within bounds:

1. To request the participation of the students in only 40 of the 80 public schools.

[4] *Ibid.*
[5] *Ibid.*

2. To draw a subsample of students in those public schools in which there were 100 or more seniors according to the most current Office of Education report. In summary, our aim was to obtain the following samples:

40 public senior high schools, students participating;
40 public senior high schools, students not participating;
10 private high schools, students participating;
10 parochial senior high schools, students participating.

The target populations for teachers and counselors were those teaching one or more courses in grades 10, 11, and 12, and those spending 20 per cent or more time in counseling with students in grades 10, 11, and 12.

The sampling procedure

A quota sampling procedure was used to select the public senior high schools.[6] The schools were selected at random from the U.S. Office of Education's *Directory of Public Secondary Day Schools, 1958–1959*. Schools were accepted for the sample as long as the quota for that particular type of school had not been filled. When the quota was filled, the schools were rejected until the number of schools needed was obtained. The Project Talent Taxonomy of Public Senior High Schools[7] provided the basis for establishing the quotas for various types of schools. The taxonomy is based on U.S. Office of Education regions, community size, and an index of the socioeconomic level of the neighborhood. The size of the senior class was also considered in selecting the schools. The categories of the Project Talent Taxonomy of High Schools are:

Code	Description
21	Cities A—low-cost housing—low income
22	Cities A—moderate and high-cost housing
31	Cities B—low-cost housing and low income
32	Cities B—moderate and high-cost housing
41	Northeast—urban—low-cost housing and low income

[6] Shaycoft, Marion F., *Stratified Random Sampling of Public Senior High Schools Stratified by Taxonomy Group, Procedure A*. Project Talent Office, University of Pittsburgh, November, 1962. Unpublished Memorandum.
[7] Flanagan, John C., and others, *op. cit.*

42   Northeast—urban—moderate and high-cost housing
43   Northeast—small town
44   Northeast—rural
51   Southeast—urban—low-cost housing and low income
52   Southeast—urban—moderate and high-cost housing
53   Southeast—small town
54   Southeast—rural
61   West—urban—low-cost housing and low income
62   West—urban—moderate and high-cost housing
63   West—small town
64   West—rural
10   All vocational high schools

Community sizes are:

Cities A—more than 1,500,000 population (1960 census),
Cities B—between 250,000 and 1,499,999 population,
Urban—between 5,000 and 249,999 population,
Small town—below 5,000 population.

In this study the following groups were combined: 21 and 31, 22 and 32, 43 and 44, 53 and 54, and 63 and 64. Group 10 was not included as this is the category for vocational high schools.

The following codes are used to designate categories of senior-class enrollments:

1—0 to 24 seniors
2—25 to 99 seniors
3—100 to 399 seniors
4—400 seniors or more

The specific procedures for selecting the public senior high schools are presented next.

Random selection of schools. A list of public senior high schools is given in the *Directory of Public Secondary Day Schools, 1958–1959,* published by the U.S. Office of Education. For purposes of random sampling, each school on the list was assumed to be identified by a six-digit number of the form XXX-X-XX. The first three digits indicate the page in which the school is listed in the *Directory;* the next digit represents the column on the page; and the last two digits represent the position of the school in the column.

A sequence of six-digit random numbers was obtained from a table of random numbers. A number was discarded if the first three digits were not in the appropriate range for the pages in the *Directory,* 011–158. The school corresponding to each random number was selected. If it turned out that there was no entry in the *Directory* corresponding to the random number, that number was discarded and the next one looked up. Similarly, if the school turned out to be one not in the population being sampled (for example, a junior high or a vocational school) it was discarded.

The group (Project Talent High School Taxonomy group and senior class size category) to which a school belonged was determined, and it was then entered in the sample if the quota for its category had not already been filled.

Determination of taxonomy group characteristics and senior class size. The size of the senior class and U.S. Office of Education region were obtained from the *Directory of Public Secondary Day Schools, 1958–1959.* City size was determined from Bureau of the Census data in *World Almanac, 1960,* using the mailing address given in the *Directory.* Schools were entered in the sample in the order in which they were drawn if the quota for the category had not been filled, but were rejected after the quota had been filled. Additional samples were selected as it was necessary to determine the socioeconomic level of the neighborhood of the school (for city schools) and additional schools would be required as replacements for rejects (that is, schools which did not meet "SES" specifications).

Two reserve samples were selected for the nonurban schools (taxonomy groups 43, 44, 53, 54, 63, and 64) and four reserve samples were selected for the urban schools (taxonomy groups 21, 22, 31, 32, 41, 42, 51, 52, and 61, 62). Four samples were selected for the urban schools since it was anticipated that some urban schools would be dropped which were not in the appropriate socioeconomic category.

The Retail Credit Company was employed to determine the socioeconomic level of the schools. Socioeconomic level of the school was defined in terms of the following item:

"The residences in the area served by the school are best described as *primarily:*

1. expensive private homes
2. moderate priced homes
3. low-cost homes

4. high-rental apartments
5. moderate-rental apartments
6. low-rental apartments
7. low-income areas
8. about equally apartments and homes
9. students are resident students—cannot estimate."

The schools were dichotomized into "low" versus "medium" and "high" socioeconomic status, using options 3, 6, and 7 versus 2, 4, 5, 8, 9. The schools were classified upon receipt of the returns from the Retail Credit Company. If it turned out that a school in the first sample drawn did not have the appropriate "SES" characteristics, the next alternate in the same taxonomy and senior class size category was selected.

Vocational schools were excluded from the sample on the basis of the school name; in addition, a check was instituted with U.S. Office of Education personnel familiar with the schools to assure that vocational schools were not included in the sample. Also excluded from the sample were schools tested by Project Talent in 1960.

Sampling the parochial high schools. A sample of 10 diocesan or parochial secondary schools was obtained through the cooperation of the National Catholic Education Association (NCEA). At our request, a list was submitted of 20 secondary schools that NCEA felt adequately represented the Roman Catholic secondary schools of the nation. Thus the method of sampling was purposive rather than statistically random. Ten schools were selected from the list of 20 for wide geographical dispersion. The Right Reverend Monsignor O'Neil C. D'Amour wrote to the Diocesan Superintendents and informed them of the purpose of the study and urged their cooperation. As a result, all of the schools invited agreed to participate in the study. Subsequently, one of the 10 schools withdrew because of scheduling difficulties. All available students in grade 10 and grade 12 in these schools were included in the sample.

Sampling the private high schools. A sample of nine private secondary schools, five male and four female, was obtained from a larger listing of these schools prepared by the Foundation staff. The schools are primarily in the East and are among those generally considered to be leading preparatory institutions. As with the parochial schools sample, the method of sampling was purposive rather than random. University of Pittsburgh staff contacted each school on the list and informed it of the purpose of the study and urged its co-operation. Repeated contacts were made until the list was exhausted. As a result, nine schools agreed to participate in the study.

Data collection

Invitations to participate in the study. A letter was sent to the school principal requesting his cooperation and that of his staff and students. An enclosure described the project briefly and the requirements in participating in the project. Briefly, the letter and enclosure emphasized the importance of obtaining objective information regarding the effects of standardized ability testing on the school's staff and on the students. In addition, a financial incentive was offered the principals in public and in private schools for their cooperation. Information copies of the letter and enclosure were sent to school superintendents in the districts in which the schools were asked to participate.

Also enclosed for their convenience in responding were a letter of reply and a stamped return envelope. The letter of reply provided space for reporting the number of students in grade 10 and in grade 12; the names of staff members spending 20 per cent or more time in counseling duties with students in grades 10, 11 and 12; the names of teachers with one or more courses in grades 10, 11 and 12; and the date on which they planned to administer the reading tests and questionnaires to the students.

Two follow-up letters were prepared. The first letter was sent to each school from two to three weeks after the mailing of the letter of invitation. The second follow-up letter was sent if a reply was not received two weeks following the mailing of the first follow-up letter. Generally, the time interval before follow-up letters were sent was affected by considerations of distance from the Washington office, greater time being given to those west of the Mississippi River than to those east of the Mississippi River. In a number of cases when replies were not received within a reasonable time following the mailing of the first or second follow-up letter, the principals were called long distance by the project director.

Administration of the reading test and students' questionnaire. The administration of the project was scheduled for January and February, 1964. For a number of schools it was necessary to permit administration of student materials in March due to scheduling difficulties. All materials for the project were sent to the school principal who was asked to act as the coordinator for the project or to appoint someone as his representative to carry out these duties. The Students' Questionnaire and Reading Test were administered by members of the school staff; the Teachers' Questionnaire and the Counselors' Questionnaire were distributed by the school principal and returned to him in sealed envelopes to preserve anonymity. The following guides were sent to the schools to provide them with information regarding procedures for the handling, administration and return of all materials:

1. Local Coordinator's Guide for the Students' Questionnaire and Reading Comprehension Test
2. Local Coordinator's Guide for the Teachers' Questionnaire and Card Sort and the Counselors' Questionnaire and Card Sort
3. The Administrator's Guide for the Students' Questionnaire and Reading Test.

Record forms were also sent to the schools in which the students were tested. The record form was to be completed by each administrator as a means of checking on proper administrative procedures.

Processing, scoring, and analyzing the data

When the data were received in the Washington office they were checked to be sure that the materials were returned that were requested in the Local Coordinator's Guides. When some materials were missing the schools were requested to testify to their security. In most cases the missing materials had been destroyed or, as far as we could tell, were mailed out but not delivered.

The Teachers' Questionnaire, Counselors' Questionnaire, and Testing Program Questionnaire were coded, key-punched, and sent to the University of Pittsburgh Data Processing and Computation Center for entry on computer tape. The Teachers' Card Sort and Counselors' Card Sort were key-punched under the direction of Russell Sage Foundation and forwarded to the Data Processing and Computation Center. Two high-speed digital computers, the IBM 7070 and the IBM 7090, were used to analyze the data.

Copies of all questionnaires used as well as local coordinators' and administrators' guides appear in Technical Report No. 3 on the Social Consequences of Testing.[8]

[8] Brim, Orville G., Jr., and others, *op. cit.*

APPENDIX II

TEACHERS' QUESTIONNAIRE

The University of Pittsburgh in conjunction with Russell Sage Foundation of New York has been given support by the U.S. Office of Education to study the consequences of ability testing in schools. Aptitude and achievement tests have sometimes been criticized on the basis of conjecture and not on scientifically established facts. It is our hope through this study to obtain accurate information about this important area.

We would greatly appreciate your cooperation in completing the following questionnaire concerning your experiences with standardized tests and your opinions about testing. We hope that you will be entirely candid in your answers to these questions.

General Directions: This questionnaire is to be completed by all teachers in grades 10, 11, and 12. It should take about forty minutes to complete. Please try to fill it out at one sitting.

When you have finished, put the questionnaire in the accompanying envelope, seal the envelope, write your name on the *outside* of the envelope, and give it to your school principal. Your responses will be kept strictly confidential.

University of Pittsburgh
Russell Sage Foundation
1964

Name of school _____

City _____ State _____

School code number _____ Date _____

Directions: Please place all of your answers in this booklet. Answer each question as accurately and as frankly as possible but do not spend too much time on any one question. Please choose the one best answer for each question. ALL ANSWERS ARE STRICTLY CONFIDENTIAL.

Answer each question as indicated; place an "X" in the parentheses to the left of the answer you choose or write your answer in the space provided. If you choose the option "other (specify)" for any question, be sure to write in your answer on the line provided as well as marking an "X" in the parentheses.

Your background

1. Sex

( ) 1. Male
( ) 2. Female

2. Age

( ) 1. 25 or under
( ) 2. 26–30
( ) 3. 31–35
( ) 4. 36–40
( ) 5. 41–45
( ) 6. 46–50
( ) 7. 51–55
( ) 8. 56–60
( ) 9. Over 60

3. Greatest amount of education completed

( ) 1. High school
( ) 2. Some college
( ) 3. Bachelor's Degree
( ) 4. Bachelor's Degree, some credit toward Master's
( ) 5. Master's Degree
( ) 6. Master's Degree, some credit toward Ph.D. or Ed.D.
( ) 7. Ph.D. or Ed.D.

4. Which of the following best describes the educational institution that awarded your highest degree?

( ) 1. Nonuniversity-affiliated teachers college
( ) 2. University-affiliated teachers college or school of education
( ) 3. University (but not in the school of education)
( ) 4. Liberal arts college
( ) 5. Other
( ) 6. No college degree

5. What was your major area of study leading to your highest degree?

( ) 1. Education
( ) 2. Guidance
( ) 3. Physical education or home economics
( ) 4. Psychology
( ) 5. Other social sciences
( ) 6. Natural sciences or mathematics
( ) 7. Humanities (English, history, etc.)
( ) 8. Languages
( ) 9. Other (specify) _____

6. Approximately how many graduate or undergraduate courses in the following general area have you had? Tests and Measurements (sample course titles: Individual Testing; Analysis of the Individual; Psychological Measurements; Diagnostic Testing; Group Tests and Techniques; Mental Measurements; Personality Testing; etc.)?

( ) 1. None
( ) 2. One
( ) 3. Two
( ) 4. Three
( ) 5. Four
( ) 6. Five or more

7. Approximately how many graduate or undergraduate courses in the following general area have

you had? Methods of research (sample course titles: Research in Education; Statistical Methods in Education and Psychology; Statistics; Educational Statistics; Methods in Educational Research; Research Design; etc.)?

( ) 1. None
( ) 2. One
( ) 3. Two
( ) 4. Three
( ) 5. Four
( ) 6. Five or more

8. How many years have you spent teaching part-time in public schools?

————————— years

9. How many years have you spent teaching full-time in public schools?

————————— years

10. How many years have you spent teaching part-time in independent schools (not parochial or public)?

————————— years

11. How many years have you spent teaching full-time in independent schools?

————————— years

12. How many years have you spent teaching part-time in parochial schools?

————————— years

13. How many years have you spent teaching full-time in parochial schools?

————————— years

14. How many years have you held your present position?

————————— years

15. Approximately what proportion of your in-school time is formally allocated at present to discussing

school problems with students or parents?

————————— per cent

16. Approximately what proportion of your in-school time do you spend discussing school problems with students or parents in addition to formally allocated hours?

————————— per cent

Questions 17–19: In which of the following areas have you had previous experience?

(1) (2)
Yes No
( ) ( ) 17. Counseling or guidance in education
( ) ( ) 18. Administrative position in education
( ) ( ) 19. Full-time position outside of education (do not include summer employment)

Questions 20–24: Which of the following kinds of students do you teach at present?

Yes No
( ) ( ) 20. College preparatory
( ) ( ) 21. Vocational
( ) ( ) 22. Special section(s) for gifted pupils
( ) ( ) 23. Special section(s) for retarded pupils
( ) ( ) 24. Other (specify) ————

25. Write in the parentheses on each line the percentage of your time given to teaching that subject. (The percentages should add to 100.)

%	Subject
( )	English
( )	Social studies
( )	Science
( )	Mathematics
( )	Foreign languages
( )	Commercial subjects (typing, shorthand, etc.)
( )	Art or Music

( ) Physical education
(___) Other (specify) _____
100 Total

Your opinions about standardized tests and their use

26. How accurate do you feel most standardized intelligence or aptitude tests are in measuring a student's potential?

( ) 1. Much better than other measures of ability (e.g., teacher evaluations, nonstandardized tests)
( ) 2. Slightly better than other measures
( ) 3. No better than other measures
( ) 4. Not so good as other measures
( ) 5. Much worse than other measures
( ) 6. No opinion

27. Which one of the following kinds of information do you feel provides the single most accurate measure of a student's intellectual ability?

( ) 1. Grade average
( ) 2. Parents' opinions
( ) 3. Standardized achievement-test scores
( ) 4. IQ or scholastic aptitude-test scores
( ) 5. Teacher recommendations
( ) 6. The student's own opinion
( ) 7. Peers' opinions

28. Which one of the following kinds of information do you feel provides the second most accurate measure of a student's intellectual ability?

( ) 1. Grade average
( ) 2. Parents' opinions
( ) 3. Standardized achievement-test scores
( ) 4. IQ or scholastic aptitude-test scores
( ) 5. Teacher recommendations
( ) 6. The student's own opinion
( ) 7. Peers' opinions

29. Which one of the following kinds of information do you feel provides the third most accurate measure of a student's intellectual ability?

( ) 1. Grade average
( ) 2. Parents' opinions
( ) 3. Standardized achievement-test scores
( ) 4. IQ or scholastic aptitude-test scores
( ) 5. Teacher recommendations
( ) 6. The student's own opinion
( ) 7. Peers' opinions

Use the following scale in answering items 30–72.

1. None
2. A very slight amount
3. A fairly slight amount
4. A moderate amount
5. A fairly great amount
6. A great amount

In questions 30–72, we should like to know how much weight you think should be given to several different kinds of information, including test scores, in making decisions about a student or advising him about his future plans.

Please answer by writing in the parentheses at the left of each question the number of the statement in the scale given above that you think best answers it.

Questions 30–35: How much weight should be given to intelligence-test scores in

( ) 30. assigning a student to an accelerated track or special class (or classes) for advanced students?
( ) 31. assigning a student to a special class (or classes) for slow students?
( ) 32. writing a recommendation for college admission or scholarship aid?
( ) 33. allowing a student to take extra courses?
( ) 34. counseling a student on occupational plans?
( ) 35. counseling a student about his choice of a college?

Questions 36–42: How much weight should be given to standardized achievement-test scores in

( ) 36. assigning a student to an accelerated track or a special class (or classes) for advanced students?
( ) 37. assigning a student to a special class (or classes) for slow students?
( ) 38. writing a recommendation for college admission or scholarship aid?
( ) 39. assigning grades?
( ) 40. allowing a student to take extra courses?
( ) 41. counseling a student on occupational plans?
( ) 42. counseling a student about his choice of a college

Questions 43–48: How much weight should be given to over-all grade average in

( ) 43. assigning a student to an accelerated track or special class (or classes) for advanced students?
( ) 44. assigning a student to a special class (or classes) for slow students?
( ) 45. writing a recommendation for college admission or scholarship aid?
( ) 46. allowing a student to take extra courses?
( ) 47. counseling a student on occupational plans?
( ) 48. counseling a student about his choice of a college?

Questions 49–54: How much weight should be given to personality-test scores in

( ) 49. assigning a student to an accelerated track or special class (or classes) for advanced students?
( ) 50. assigning a student to a special class (or classes) for slow students?
( ) 51. writing a recommendation for college admission or scholarship aid?

( ) 52. allowing a student to take extra courses?
( ) 53. counseling a student on occupational plans?
( ) 54. counseling a student about his choice of a college?

Questions 55–60: How much weight should be given to vocational-interest-inventory scores in

( ) 55. assigning a student to an accelerated track or a special class (or classes) for advanced students?
( ) 56. assigning a student to a special class (or classes) for slow students?
( ) 57. writing a recommendation for college admission or scholarship aid?
( ) 58. allowing a student to take extra courses?
( ) 59. counseling a student on occupational plans?
( ) 60. counseling a student about his choice of a college?

Questions 61–66: How much weight should be given to recommendations of former teachers in

( ) 61. assigning a student to an accelerated track or a special class (or classes) for advanced students?
( ) 62. assigning a student to a special class (or classes) for slow students?
( ) 63. writing a recommendation for college admission or scholarship aid?
( ) 64. allowing a student to take extra courses?
( ) 65. counseling a student on occupational plans?
( ) 66. counseling a student about his choice of a college?

Questions 67–72: How much weight should be given to information about a student's family background (e.g., father's occupation, financial status, etc.) in

( ) 67. assigning a student to an accelerated track or a special class (or classes) for advanced students?

( ) 68. assigning a student to a special class (or classes) for slow students?

( ) 69. writing a recommendation for college admission or scholarship aid?

( ) 70. allowing a student to take extra courses?

( ) 71. counseling a student on occupational plans?

( ) 72. counseling a student on his choice of a college?

73. In cases where a student's aptitude or IQ scores are considerably <u>higher</u> than other indications of his ability (e.g., grades, achievement-test scores), what effect would this be likely to have on the amount of weight you would give to the IQ scores in making decisions like those specified in the preceding questions?

( ) 1. Considerably more weight
( ) 2. Slightly more weight
( ) 3. Slightly less weight
( ) 4. Considerably less weight
( ) 5. It woulld probably not have any effect.
( ) 6. I don't know.

74. In cases where a student's aptitude or IQ scores are considerably <u>lower</u> than other indications of his ability (e.g., grades, achievement-test scores), what effect would this be likely to have on the amount of weight you would give to the IQ scores in making decisions like those given in the preceding questions?

( ) 1. Considerably more weight
( ) 2. Slightly more weight
( ) 3. Slightly less weight
( ) 4. Considerably less weight
( ) 5. It would probably not have any effect.
( ) 6. I don't know.

75. How do you feel about the use of standardized achievement-test scores by school administrators for evaluating the effectiveness of teachers?

( ) 1. This is almost always the best way of evaluating a teacher's effectiveness.

( ) 2. This is sometimes the best way of evaluating a teacher's effectiveness.

( ) 3. This is a relatively poor way of evaluating a teacher's effectiveness.

( ) 4. Achievement-test scores should never be used for evaluating a teacher's effectiveness.

Your opinions about SCHOOL-SPONSORED *standardized testing and* EXTERNALLY SPONSORED *testing*

76. How do you feel about the number of <u>school-sponsored</u> standardized tests that are given in your school?

( ) 1. Far too many tests are given.
( ) 2. Too many tests are given.
( ) 3. About the right number of tests are given.
( ) 4. Too few tests are given.
( ) 5. Far too few tests are given.
( ) 6. No opinion

77. How do you feel about the amount of use that is made of scores on <u>school-sponsored</u> standardized tests <u>in your school</u>?

( ) 1. Much more use should be made of test scores.
( ) 2. Slightly more use should be made of test scores.
( ) 3. About the right amount of use is being made of test scores.
( ) 4. Slightly less use should be made of test scores.
( ) 5. Much less use should be made of test scores.
( ) 6. No opinion

78. How do you feel about the <u>ways</u> in which scores on <u>school-sponsored</u> standardized tests are being used in your school?

( ) 1. Very different uses should be made of test scores.
( ) 2. Slightly different uses should be made of test scores.

( ) 3. Test scores are used in about the right ways.

( ) 4. No opinion

79. How do you feel about the number of externally sponsored tests that are given in your school?

( ) 1. Far too many externally sponsored tests are given.

( ) 2. Too many tests are given.

( ) 3. About the right number of tests are given.

( ) 4. Too few tests are given.

( ) 5. Far too few tests are given.

( ) 6. No opinion

Familiarity with standardized tests

Use the following scale in answering questions 80–95.

1. I have never heard of the test.
2. I recognize the name but have no other knowledge about the test.
3. I know what the test measures only in a general way.
4. I have examined (or studied about) the test and am familiar with it.

For questions 80–95, write in the parentheses at the left of each test title the number of the statement in the scale given above that best indicates your degree of familiarity with the test. Be sure to write in a number for each test.

( ) 80. Stanford-Binet Intelligence Test

( ) 81. Wechsler Intelligence Scales

( ) 82. Bell Adjustment Inventory

( ) 83. Strong Vocational Interest Blanks

( ) 84. Differential Aptitude Tests

( ) 85. Minnesota Multiphasic Personality Inventory

( ) 86. Kuder Preference Record, Vocational Form C

( ) 87. California Test of Mental Maturity

( ) 88. California Test of Personality

( ) 89. Otis Quick-Scoring Test of Mental Ability

( ) 90. Lorge-Thorndike Intelligence Tests

( ) 91. Iowa Tests of Educational Development

( ) 92. School and College Ability Test (SCAT)

( ) 93. Sequential Tests of Educational Progress (STEP)

( ) 94. College Board Scholastic Aptitude Test (SAT)

( ) 95. Preliminary Scholastic Aptitude Test (PSAT)

Directions: Place an "X" in the parentheses corresponding to the answer you choose for each question.

96. Have you ever seen a copy of the booklet, A Description of the College Board Scholastic Aptitude Test (published by Educational Testing Service)?

( ) 1. Yes, a copy of each year's edition is distributed to teachers in our school.

( ) 2. Yes.

( ) 3. No, but I have often wondered how I might get a copy.

( ) 4. No, this is the first time I have seen a reference to the booklet.

( ) 5. No.

97. Have you ever taken the SAT?

( ) 1. Yes, more than once.

( ) 2. Yes, once.

( ) 3. I don't think so.

( ) 4. No.

( ) 5. I don't know.

98. Have you ever examined a complete copy (not just sample questions) of the College Board Scholastic Aptitude Test (SAT)? Do not count your own pre-college experience in taking the SAT.

( ) 1. Yes, within the past two years.

( ) 2. Yes, prior to two years ago.

( ) 3. Yes, both within the past two years and prior to that.

( ) 4. I don't think so.

( ) 5. No.

( ) 6. I don't know.

99. Have you ever examined a complete copy of the Preliminary Scholastic Aptitude Test (PSAT), which is administered in many

schools in October of each school year?

( ) 1. Yes, within the past two years.
( ) 2. Yes, prior to two years ago.
( ) 3. Yes, both within the past two years and prior to that.
( ) 4. I don't think so.
( ) 5. No.
( ) 6. I don't know.

100. Have you ever examined a complete copy of the National Merit Scholarship Qualifying Test?

( ) 1. Yes, within the past two years.
( ) 2. Yes, prior to two years ago.
( ) 3. Yes, both within the past two years and prior to that.
( ) 4. I don't think so.
( ) 5. No.
( ) 6. I don't know.

101. Have you ever examined a complete copy of any of the tests in the American College Testing program?

( ) 1. Yes, within the past two years.
( ) 2. Yes, prior to two years ago.
( ) 3. Yes, both within the past two years and prior to that.
( ) 4. I don't think so.
( ) 5. No.
( ) 6. I don't know.

102. Have you ever examined a complete copy of any of the College Board achievement tests?

( ) 1. Yes, within the past two years.
( ) 2. Yes, prior to two years ago.
( ) 3. Yes, both within the past two years and prior to that.
( ) 4. I don't think so.
( ) 5. No.
( ) 6. I don't know.

103. Have you ever seen a complete copy of any other standardized achievement tests (for example, the Iowa Tests of Educational Development)?

( ) 1. Yes, within the past two years.
( ) 2. Yes, prior to two years ago.
( ) 3. Yes, both within the past two years and prior to that.

( ) 4. I don't think so.
( ) 5. No.
( ) 6. I don't know.

Questions 104–109: Which of the following kinds of tests have you personally administered at least once since you began teaching? (Be sure to mark an answer for each type of test.)

(1) (2)
Yes No
( ) ( ) 104. Group intelligence test (e.g., Otis or Lorge-Thorndike)
( ) ( ) 105. Standardized achievement test (e.g., Iowa Tests of Educational Development)
( ) ( ) 106. Individual intelligence test (e.g., Stanford-Binet or Wechsler)
( ) ( ) 107. Vocational-interest inventory (e.g., Kuder)
( ) ( ) 108. Personality or adjustment inventory
( ) ( ) 109. Standardized aptitude test (e.g., DAT)

Questions 110–115: Which of the following kinds of tests are you routinely responsible for administering every year (or every other year)? (Be sure to mark an answer for each type of test.)

(1) (2)
Yes No
( ) ( ) 110. Group intelligence test
( ) ( ) 111. Standardized achievement test
( ) ( ) 112. Individual intelligence test
( ) ( ) 113. Vocational-interest inventory
( ) ( ) 114. Personality or adjustment inventory
( ) ( ) 115. Standardized aptitude test

Questions 116–121: Which of the following kinds of tests have you been responsible for scoring at least once since you began teaching? (Be sure to mark an answer for each type of test.)

(1) (2)
Yes No
( ) ( ) 116. Group intelligence test
( ) ( ) 117. Standardized achievement test
( ) ( ) 118. Individual intelligence test
( ) ( ) 119. Vocational-interest inventory
( ) ( ) 120. Personality or adjustment inventory
( ) ( ) 121. Standardized aptitude test

Questions 122–127: Which of the following kinds of tests have you been routinely responsible for scoring? (Be sure to mark an answer for each type of test.)

(1) (2)
Yes No
( ) ( ) 122. Group intelligence test
( ) ( ) 123. Standardized achievement test
( ) ( ) 124. Individual intelligence test
( ) ( ) 125. Vocational-interest inventory
( ) ( ) 126. Personality or adjustment inventory
( ) ( ) 127. Standardized aptitude test

Access to standardized test scores

Use the following scale in answering questions 128–132.

1. No opinion
2. No, teachers should never see these scores.
3. Teachers should be allowed to see these scores only under special circumstances.
4. Teachers should have access to these scores whenever they wish.
5. Yes, teachers should receive these scores routinely.

For questions 128–132, write in the parentheses at the left of each question the number of the statement in the scale given above that best expresses your answer to it.

( ) 128. Do you feel that teachers ought to have their pupils' IQ scores?

( ) 129. Do you feel that teachers ought to have college-admissions test scores (e.g., SAT or ACT)?

( ) 130. Do you feel that teachers ought to have their pupils' scores on standardized achievement tests (like the Iowa Tests of Educational Development)?

( ) 131. Do you feel that teachers ought to have their pupils' scores on vocational-interest inventories given by the school?

( ) 132. Do you feel that teachers ought to have their pupils' scores on personailty tests given by the school?

133. Do you think teachers should ever give a high-school student specific information about his intelligence (e.g., either his IQ or its percentile rank)?

( ) 1. Yes, to most or all students whether the student asks for it or not.
( ) 2. Yes, to any pupils that ask about it.
( ) 3. Yes, to some students whether or not they ask about it.
( ) 4. Yes, to some students if they ask about it.
( ) 5. Only under special circumstances.
( ) 6. No, never.
( ) 7. No opinion

134. Do you think teachers should ever give a high-school student general information about his intelligence (e.g., a general idea of where he stands relative to the other pupils in his class)?

( ) 1. Yes, to most or all students whether the student asks for it or not.
( ) 2. Yes, to any pupils who ask about it.
( ) 3. Yes, to some students whether or not they ask about it.
( ) 4. Yes, to some students if they ask about it.
( ) 5. Only under special circumstances.
( ) 6. No, never.

135. Do you think teachers should ever give a pupil's <u>parents specific information</u> about the pupil's intelligence (e.g., his IQ or its percentile rank)?

( ) 1. Yes, to most or all parents.
( ) 2. Yes, to any parent that asks about it.
( ) 3. Yes, to some parents whether or not they ask about it.
( ) 4. Yes, to some parents if they ask about it.
( ) 5. Only under special circumstances.
( ) 6. No, never.
( ) 7. No opinion

136. Do you think teachers should ever give a pupil's <u>parents general information</u> about the pupil's intelligence (e.g., a general idea of where the student stands relative to the other pupils in his class)?

( ) 1. Yes, to most or all parents.
( ) 2. Yes, to any parent that asks about it.
( ) 3. Yes, to some parents whether or not they ask about it.
( ) 4. Yes, to some parents if they ask about it.
( ) 5. Only under special circumstances.
( ) 6. No, never.
( ) 7. No opinion

Use the following scale in answering questions 137–142.

| 1. No, my pupils don't take this test. |
| 2. No, I have <u>never known</u> any of my pupils' scores. |
| 3. Yes, although I <u>do not normally have access</u> to these scores, I have sometimes known one of my pupil's scores. |
| 4. Yes, I have access to these scores and I <u>occasionally</u> look at the records. |
| 5. Yes, I have access to these scores and I <u>frequently</u> look at the records. |
| 6. Yes, I <u>routinely receive</u> most or all of these scores. |

For questions 137–142, write in the parentheses at the left of each question the number of the statement in the scale given above that best expresses your answer to it.

( ) 137. Have you ever known any of your pupils' <u>intelligence-test</u> scores?
( ) 138. Have you ever known any of your pupils' <u>college-admissions</u> test scores (SAT or ACT)?
( ) 139. Have you ever known any of your pupils' National Merit Scholarship Qualifying Test scores?
( ) 140. Have you ever known any of your pupils' scores on any standardized achievement tests (like the Iowa Tests of Educational Development) given by your school?
( ) 141. Have you ever known any of your pupils' scores on <u>vocational-interest</u> inventories given by your school?
( ) 142. Have you ever known any of your pupils' scores on personality tests given by your school?

143. Have you ever given a student <u>specific information</u> about his intelligence (either his IQ or its percentile rank)?

( ) 1. Yes, to <u>most</u> or <u>all</u> of my pupils.
( ) 2. Yes, to <u>many</u> students.
( ) 3. Yes, to <u>some</u> students.
( ) 4. Yes, to <u>a few</u> students.
( ) 5. No. Although I have access to my pupils' intelligence-test scores, I have never given any of them specific information about their intelligence.
( ) 6. No, I do not have access to my pupils' intelligence-test scores.

144. Have you ever given a pupil <u>general information</u> about his intelligence (e.g., a general idea of where he stands relative to the other pupils in his class)?

( ) 1. Yes, to <u>most</u> or <u>all</u> of my students.
( ) 2. Yes, to <u>many</u> students.

( ) 3. Yes, to some students.
( ) 4. Yes, to a few students.
( ) 5. No. Although I have access to my pupils' intelligence-test scores, I have never given them general information about their intelligence.
( ) 6. No, I do not have access to my pupils' intelligence-test scores.

145. Have you ever given a parent specific information about his child's intelligence (e.g., either an IQ or its percentile rank)?

( ) 1. Yes, to most or all of my students' parents.
( ) 2. Yes, to many parents.
( ) 3. Yes, to some parents.
( ) 4. Yes, to a few parents.
( ) 5. No. Although I have access to my pupils' intelligence-test scores, I have never given a parent specific information about his child's intelligence.
( ) 6. No, I do not have access to my pupils' intelligence-test scores.

146. Have you ever given a parent general information about his child's intelligence?

( ) 1. Yes, to most or all of my students' parents.
( ) 2. Yes, to many parents.
( ) 3. Yes, to some parents.
( ) 4. Yes, to a few parents.
( ) 5. No. Although I have access to my pupils' intelligence-test scores, I have never given a parent general information about his child's intelligence.
( ) 6. No, I do not have access to my pupils' intelligence-test scores.

147. In general, do you feel that you have an accurate estimate of how intelligent your students are?

( ) 1. Yes, I am fairly sure I know how intelligent all of my students are.
( ) 2. Yes, I am fairly sure I know how intelligent most of my students are.
( ) 3. I am fairly sure I know how intelligent a few of my students are.

( ) 4. No, I do not know how intelligent any of my students are.

148. Do you feel that your students have an accurate estimate of how intelligent they are?

( ) 1. Yes, all of my students have a fairly accurate estimate.
( ) 2. Yes, most have a fairly accurate estimate.
( ) 3. A few of my students have a fairly accurate estimate.
( ) 4. No. None of my students has a fairly accurate estimate.
( ) 5. I don't know.

149. Have you ever had a student indicate to you that he did not know how intelligent he was?

( ) 1. Frequently
( ) 2. Occasionally
( ) 3. Rarely
( ) 4. Never
( ) 5. I don't remember.

150. How often do your students ask you for information about their abilities?

( ) 1. Frequently
( ) 2. Occasionally
( ) 3. Rarely
( ) 4. Never

151. How frequently do parents of your students ask you for information about their children's abilities?

( ) 1. Frequently
( ) 2. Occasionally
( ) 3. Rarely
( ) 4. Never

152. In general, about how many of the parents you come in contact with have a good idea of how intelligent their children are?

( ) 1. All or nearly all
( ) 2. Most
( ) 3. Some
( ) 4. None
( ) 5. I don't know.

153. Do you feel that teachers, counselors, psychologists, etc. should give high-school students specific

information concerning their intelligence (e.g., IQ's or their percentile ranks)?

( ) 1. All students should be given specific information routinely.
( ) 2. Most students should be given specific information.
( ) 3. Only in special cases
( ) 4. No students should ever be given specific information.
( ) 5. No opinion

Use of standardized-test scores

Use the following scale in answering questions 154–157.

1. I don't know.
2. No, I do not have access to these scores.
3. No. Although I have access to these scores, I have never used them for this.
4. Yes, occasionally.
5. Yes, frequently.
6. Yes, always or nearly always.

For questions 154–157, write in the parentheses at the left of each question the number of the statement in the scale given above that best expresses your answer to it.

( ) 154. Have you ever used a pupil's intelligence-test score as one basis for assigning him a grade in one of your classes?
( ) 155. Have you ever considered a pupil's college-admissions test scores as one basis for assigning him a grade in one of your classes?
( ) 156. Have you ever made use of a pupil's intelligence-test score in advising him about his work in your course (or other courses)?
( ) 157. Have you ever made use of a pupil's college-admissions test score in advising him about his work in your course (or other courses)?

158. Do you think that a teacher should take into account the average intelligence level of a class

when she sets the passing mark in assigning grades?

( ) 1. Yes, always or nearly always.
( ) 2. Yes, frequently.
( ) 3. Only in special cases.
( ) 4. No, never.
( ) 5. No opinion

159. Do you think that a teacher should take into account the average college-admissions test scores of a class when she sets the passing mark in assigning grades?

( ) 1. Yes, always or nearly always.
( ) 2. Yes, frequently.
( ) 3. Only in special cases.
( ) 4. No, never.
( ) 5. No opinion

(1) (2)   *Preparation for tests*

Yes No
( ) ( ) 160. Have you ever prepared students for a standardized test by teaching them shortly in advance of the test administration specific information you knew was included in the test?
( ) ( ) 161. Have you ever prepared students for a standardized test by teaching them shortly in advance of the test administration how to take such tests (how to distribute their time wisely, whether to mark answers to all questions, etc.)?
( ) ( ) 162. Have you ever prepared students for a standardized test by emphasizing over a considerable period of time the kind of subject matter covered by the test (without any knowledge about specific test items)?

Directions: In answering the following questions, we would like you to consider "preparing students specifically for taking standardized tests" as referring to any situation in which you made a conscious effort to improve your pupils' performance on a standardized test either through emphasizing subject matter that you thought might be covered on the test or by giving instruction in how to take tests or answer specific types of questions.

163. Have.you ever made an effort to prepare your classes specifically for taking standardized achievement tests (e.g., the Iowa Tests of Educational Development or the College Board achievement tests)?

( ) 1. Yes, a major part of at least one of the courses I teach is designed specifically for this purpose.

( ) 2. Yes, a minor part of at least one of the courses I teach is for this purpose.

( ) 3. Yes, occasionally.

( ) 4. No, never.

164. Have you ever made an effort to prepare your classes specifically for taking aptitude or intelligence tests (e.g., the Scholastic Aptitude Test of the College Board)?

( ) 1. Yes, a major part of at least one of the courses I teach is designed specifically to prepare students for one or both of these tests.

( ) 2. Yes, a minor part of at least one of the courses I teach is for this purpose.

( ) 3. Yes, occasionally.

( ) 4. No, never.

Use the following scale in answering questions 165–169.

| 1. Yes, frequently |
| 2. Yes, occasionally |
| 3. Yes, once or twice |
| 4. No, never |

For questions 165–169, write in the parentheses at the left of each question the number of the statement in the scale given above that best expresses your answer to it.

( ) 165. Have you ever made an effort to prepare any of your pupils specifically for standardized achievement tests on an individual basis in school?

( ) 166. Have you ever made an effort to prepare any of your pupils specifically for standardized achievement tests on an individual basis outside school?

( ) 167. Have you ever made an effort to prepare any of your pupils specifically for scholastic aptitude or intelligence tests on an individual basis in school?

( ) 168. Have you ever made an effort to prepare any of your pupils specifically for scholastic aptitude or intelligence tests on an individual basis outside school?

( ) 169. Have you ever conducted a special class designed to prepare students specifically for standardized tests?

170. Has your knowledge of the content of one or more standardized achievement tests in your field ever caused you to alter the content of the courses taught by you?

( ) 1. Yes, on several occasions.

( ) 2. Yes, on a few occasions.

( ) 3. Yes, on one occasion.

( ) 4. No.

( ) 5. I have no knowledge of the content of any standardized achievement test in my field.

( ) 6. I don't know.

171. Has your knowledge of the content of one or more standardized achievement tests in your field ever caused you to change your teaching methods (but not the content of your courses)?

( ) 1. Yes, on several occasions.

( ) 2. Yes, on a few occasions.

( ) 3. Yes, on one or two occasions.

( ) 4. No.

( ) 5. I have no knowledge of the content of any standardized achievement test in my field.

( ) 6. I don't know.

172. If you were to discover that a standardized achievement test which is used for college admission differed in its emphasis on your field from the present content of your courses in this subject, do you feel that you would change your course in any way? (Assume that you were free to do so.)

( ) 1. Definitely
( ) 2. Probably
( ) 3. Probably not
( ) 4. Definitely not
( ) 5. I don't know.

Use the following scale in answering questions 173–183.

---

1. The school has no guidance counselor.
2. I don't know or can't remember.
3. No.
4. Yes, on one or two occasions.
5. Yes, on a few occasions.
6. Yes, on several occasions.

Please answer by writing in the parentheses at the left of each question the number of the statement in the scale given above that best expresses your answer to it.

( ) 173. Have you ever been requested by the guidance counselor in your school to alter the content of any of your courses so that your students will be better prepared for standardized tests?

( ) 174. Have you ever been requested by the guidance counselor in your school to change your teaching methods or the order in which you present your material (but not the content of your courses) so that your students would be better prepared for standardized tests?

( ) 175. Have you ever been asked by the guidance counselor in your school to conduct one or more special classes designed to prepare pupils specifically for standardized tests?

( ) 176. Have you ever been asked by the principal or other administrative official of your school to alter the content of any of your courses so that your students would be better prepared for standardized tests?

( ) 177. Have you ever been asked by the principal or other administrative official of your school to change your teaching methods or the order in which you present your material (but not the content of your courses) so that your students would be better prepared for standardized tests?

( ) 178. Have you ever been asked by the parents of any of your pupils to alter the content of any of your courses so that your students would be better prepared for standardized tests?

( ) 179. Have you ever been asked by the parents of any of your pupils to change your teaching methods or the order in which you present your material (but not the content of your courses) so that your students would be better prepared for standardized tests?

( ) 180. Have you ever been asked by any of your pupils to alter the content of any of your courses so that they would be better prepared for standardized tests?

( ) 181. Have you ever been asked by any of your pupils to change your teaching methods or the order in which you present your material (but not the content of your courses) so that they would be better prepared for standardized tests?

( ) 182. Have you ever been asked by the principal or other administrative official of your school to conduct one or more special classes designed to prepare pupils specifically for standardized tests?

( ) 183. Have you ever been asked by the parents of any of your pupils to conduct one or more special classes designed to prepare pupils specifically for standardized tests?

184. Have you ever attended any clinics or meetings intended primarily to acquaint teachers with the content, philosophy, or methodology of standardized testing (not counting courses taken in college or graduate school)?

( ) 1. Yes, within the past two years.
( ) 2. Yes, prior to the past two years.
( ) 3. Yes, both within the past two years and prior to that.
( ) 4. Never.
( ) 5. I don't remember.

185. Do you feel that teachers have a responsibility to try to prepare their students specifically for standardized achievement tests (e.g., the Iowa Tests of Educational Development or the College Board achievement tests)?

( ) 1. Yes, this is a major responsibility of a teacher.
( ) 2. Yes, this is a minor responsibility of a teacher.
( ) 3. Only in some cases.
( ) 4. No.
( ) 5. I have no opinion.

186. Do you feel that teachers have a responsibility to try to prepare their students specifically for standardized aptitude or intelligence tests (e.g., the College Board Scholastic Aptitude Test)?

( ) 1. Yes, this is a major responsibility of a teacher.
( ) 2. Yes, this is a minor responsibility of a teacher.
( ) 3. Only in some cases.
( ) 4. No.
( ) 5. I have no opinion.

187. How frequently do you use objective (that is, multiple-choice, true-false, matching, or comple-

tion) questions in tests that you prepare for your students?

( ) 1. Always or nearly always
( ) 2. Most of the time
( ) 3. Frequently
( ) 4. Occasionally
( ) 5. Never or almost never

188. How frequently do you use essay or short essay questions in tests that you prepare for your students?

( ) 1. Always or nearly always
( ) 2. Most of the time
( ) 3. Frequently
( ) 4. Occasionally
( ) 5. Never or almost never

Your opinions about the nature and importance of intellectual ability

Use the following scale in answering questions 189–191.

1. No opinion
2. It is not important at all.
3. It is less important than most other qualities.
4. It is about the same in importance as most other qualities.
5. It is more important than most other qualities.
6. It is the most important quality for success.

For questions 189–191, write in the parentheses at the left of each question the number of the statement in the scale given above that best expresses your answer to the question.

( ) 189. How important do you feel the kind of intelligence measured by standardized tests is for success in school or college?

( ) 190. How important do you feel the kind of intelligence measured by standardized tests is for success in one of the professions, such as law or medicine?

( ) 191. How important do you feel the kind of intelligence measured by standardized tests is for success in the business world?

192. Do you think standardized intelligence tests measure primarily the intelligence people are born with, or what they have learned?

( ) 1. IQ tests measure only inborn intelligence.
( ) 2. IQ tests measure mostly inborn intelligence but learning makes some difference.
( ) 3. IQ tests measure inborn intelligence and learning about equally.
( ) 4. IQ tests measure mostly learned knowledge, but inborn intelligence makes some difference.
( ) 5. IQ tests measure only learned knowledge.
( ) 6. No opinion

Use the following scale in answering questions 193–196.

1. They are completely different.
2. They are more different than alike.
3. They are similar, but there are many differences.
4. They are basically the same, but there are a few differences.
6. They are identical.

For questions 193–196, write in the parentheses at the left of each question the number of the statement in the scale given above that best expresses your answer to it.

( ) 193. Do you feel that there are differences between the kind of intelligence measured by standardized tests and the kind of intelligence necessary for success in college?

( ) 194. Do you feel that there are differences between the kind of intelligence measured by standardized tests and the kind of intelligence necessary for success in graduate school?

( ) 195. Do you feel that there are differences between the kind of intelligence measured by standardized tests and the kind of intelligence necessary for success in one of the professions, such as law or medicine?

( ) 196. Do you feel that there are differences between the kind of intelligence measured by standardized tests and the kind of intelligence necessary for success in the business world?

Please go on to the Teachers' Card Sort on the next page.

TEACHERS' CARD SORT

General Directions: Assume that you are beginning the academic year as a classroom teacher in a school where you have not taught before. Each teacher is assigned a home-room and is largely responsible for the guidance counseling of the students in it. Your home-room group is made up of 28 eleventh-grade students.

Your first task as a home-room teacher is to make recommendations to the principal regarding which of the students in your class should be placed in the accelerated eleventh-grade science class and which of them should be placed in the regular eleventh-grade science class.

Detailed directions about what you are to do are given on the next page.

DIRECTIONS

Your school keeps a record card for each student on which are entered his IQ score, his percentile ranks on several well-known achievement tests in a representative sample of American school children, and his percentile ranks on nine interest areas derived from the *Kuder Preference Record,* Vocational Form C. The higher a student's percentile rank, the higher his standing in relation to the norms sample.

This record also provides evaluations of the student made by his or her adviser. The advisers are teachers of long experience who have had some training in educational and vocational guidance.

On each of the following pages you will see reproductions of these record cards for each of two eleventh-grade students. The pupil's name,* his age, and his grade level at the time the record card was filled out are given at the top of each record card. All of these cards were filled out at the end of grade 10. The data on them were obtained during each student's tenth-grade year.

Your task is to decide on the basis of the data about each of the 28 students whether he should be assigned to the accelerated science class or the regular science class in grade 11. In the accelerated class, the students are expected to learn at a faster pace and more intensively than in the regular class.

You should examine the information about each student, decide whether to recommend the accelerated or regular class for him, and indicate your decision by making an "X" on the corresponding line in the upper right-hand corner of his record card.

You may take as much time as you wish and place as many students as you wish in either science class.

* The names of all pupils are fictitious.

A

| YEARLY RECORD FOR GRADE 10 | | | Accelerated Science ____ |
| NAME Gregory Barton   AGE: 16 | | | Regular Class ____ |

Intelligence Test	IQ	Achievement Test	Percentile Rank	Kuder Interest Area	Percentile Rank
		Reading	65	Mechanical	75
		Science	89	Computational	87
		Math	88	Scientific	83
		Social Studies	64	Persuasive	64
				Artistic	50
				Literary	43
				Musical	36
				Social Service	28
				Clerical	19

HOME-ROOM TEACHER: An excellent student high in achievement and ability.

ADVISER: Well-liked. Capable. Conscientious. Excellent student.

B

| YEARLY RECORD FOR GRADE 10 | | | Accelerated Science ____ |
| NAME Glen Chapman   AGE: 16 | | | Regular Class ____ |

Intelligence Test	IQ	Achievement Test	Percentile Rank	Kuder Interest Area	Percentile Rank
California Test of Mental Maturity:	109	Reading	26	Mechanical	23
		Science	25	Computational	21
		Math	26	Scientific	18
		Social Studies	24	Persuasive	41
				Artistic	63
				Literary	61
				Musical	48
				Social Service	83
				Clerical	87

HOME-ROOM TEACHER: Glen has his heart set on becoming a scientist like his father. Unfortunately his ability does not seem to warrant this. He accompanies his father to the lab evenings and weekends and loves every minute of it. He works very hard but does not seem to understand basic scientific concepts.

ADVISER: Glen is keenly interested in all things scientific. All three science teachers have commented to me on his interest but they are worried that his ability is just not up to his ambitions.

A

YEARLY RECORD FOR GRADE __10__				Accelerated Science ____
NAME __Doris Sheehan__		AGE: __16__		Regular Class ____

Intelligence Test	IQ	Achievement Test	Percentile Rank	Kuder Interest Area	Percentile Rank
OTIS:	124	Reading	84		
		Science	82		
		Math	81		
		Social Studies	84		

HOME-ROOM TEACHER: This girl has no interest in anything but athletics. She spends all of her time in the gym. Her English teacher tells me she writes nearly all of her papers on games and sports.

ADVISER: Interested only in sports. I have talked with her about becoming a physical education teacher but she says she wants to "play," not "teach."

B

YEARLY RECORD FOR GRADE __10__				Accelerated Science ____
NAME __John Dewitt__		AGE: __16__		Regular Class ____

Intelligence Test	IQ	Achievement Test	Percentile Rank	Kuder Interest Area	Percentile Rank
California Test of Mental Maturity:	106	Reading	39		
		Science	26		
		Math	27		
		Social Studies	44		

HOME-ROOM TEACHER: John cares only for science. He is never happier than when he is "experimenting" in the little laboratory he built in his basement at home.

ADVISER: Very interested in science. He told me that his chief problem was to decide which field of science to go into.

A

YEARLY RECORD FOR GRADE __10__					Accelerated Science ____	
NAME __Mary Mullen__			AGE: __16__		Regular Class ____	

Intelligence Test	IQ	Achievement Test	Percentile Rank	Kuder Interest Area	Percentile Rank
OTIS:	129			Mechanical	26
				Computational	29
				Scientific	32
				Persuasive	43
				Artistic	76
				Literary	54
				Musical	40
				Social Service	65
				Clerical	94

HOME-ROOM TEACHER: Every teacher who has this girl complains about her. She is near the bottom in all her classes; her work is rarely handed in on time; she practically refuses to recite or to answer when called on.

ADVISER: I am concerned about Mary. She has no interest, no plans, no ambitions. She dislikes school intensely and refuses to work at anything. A very difficult girl.

B

YEARLY RECORD FOR GRADE __10__					Accelerated Science ____	
NAME __Elaine Humphrey__			AGE: __16__		Regular Class ____	

Intelligence Test	IQ	Achievement Test	Percentile Rank	Kuder Interest Area	Percentile Rank
California Test of Mental Maturity:	120	Reading	81	Mechanical	85
		Science	82	Computational	87
		Math	82	Scientific	85
		Social Studies	84	Persuasive	16
				Artistic	49
				Literary	37
				Musical	43
				Social Service	21
				Clerical	31

HOME-ROOM TEACHER:

ADVISER:

A

| YEARLY RECORD FOR GRADE __10__ | | | | Accelerated Science ____ |
| NAME __Margaret Hilton__ | | AGE: __16__ | | Regular Class ____ |

Intelligence Test	IQ	Achievement Test	Percentile Rank	Kuder Interest Area	Percentile Rank
California Test of Mental Maturity:	103			Mechanical	82
				Computational	81
				Scientific	79
				Persuasive	58
				Artistic	42
				Literary	46
				Musical	48
				Social Service	60
				Clerical	22

HOME-ROOM TEACHER: Excellent student. The math teacher tells me that he has yet to call on Margaret for an explanation that she cannot provide.

ADVISER: A born mathematician. Bright and capable girl. Will do well in any type of scientific research.

B

| YEARLY RECORD FOR GRADE __10__ | | | | Accelerated Science ____ |
| NAME __Margaret Nielson__ | | AGE: __16__ | | Regular Class ____ |

Intelligence Test	IQ	Achievement Test	Percentile Rank	Kuder Interest Area	Percentile Rank
California Test of Mental Maturity:	109	Reading	23	Mechanical	21
		Science	26	Computational	17
		Math	24	Scientific	26
		Social Studies	26	Persuasive	40
				Artistic	37
				Literary	59
				Musical	63
				Social Service	25
				Clerical	87

HOME-ROOM TEACHER: Margaret is a capable and industrious student. She does good work in all her classes and is very popular with both her teachers and her peers.

ALVISER: This girl has yet to make a firm decision regarding her future. Her chief interest lies in working in a hospital, but she does not want to become a nurse. I have discussed the possibilities of her becoming a laboratory technician, an X-ray technician, or doing medical research. Of these she prefers the last. Her interest and capability in science would make this a good choice for her.

A

YEARLY RECORD FOR GRADE __10__				Accelerated Science ____	
NAME __Mildred Learch__		AGE: __16__		Regular Class ____	
Intelligence Test	IQ	Achievement Test	Percentile Rank	Kuder Interest Area	Percentile Rank
California Test of Mental Maturity:	106	Reading	23	Mechanical	67
		Science	25	Computational	81
		Math	23	Scientific	93
		Social Studies	26	Persuasive	63
				Artistic	39
				Literary	41
				Musical	16
				Social Service	32
				Clerical	19

HOME-ROOM TEACHER: A superior student. Does excellent work in all of her classes.

ADVISER: One of our better students. No definite plans other than "college" as yet.

B

YEARLY RECORD FOR GRADE __10__				Accelerated Science ____	
NAME __Ruth Skillman__		AGE: __16__		Regular Class ____	
Intelligence Test	IQ	Achievement Test	Percentile Rank	Kuder Interest Area	Percentile Rank
California Test of Mental Maturity:	106	Reading	73	Mechanical	88
		Science	85	Computational	81
		Math	88	Scientific	84
		Social Studies	76	Persuasive	48
				Artistic	53
				Literary	41
				Musical	37
				Social Service	47
				Clerical	55

HOME-ROOM TEACHER: This girl's ability is quite high. On two different occasions teachers have told me that when class discussion gets involved she can ask a question that cuts right to the heart of the matter.

ADVISER: This girl wants to become a high-school teacher and I have encouraged her in this. She is of superior ability and I believe she will be quite successful in working with students.

A

| YEARLY RECORD FOR GRADE __10__ | | | | Accelerated Science ____ |
| NAME __Martin Anderson__ | | AGE: __16__ | | Regular Class ____ |

Intelligence Test	IQ	Achievement Test	Percentile Rank	Kuder Interest Area	Percentile Rank
California Test of Mental Maturity:	121				

HOME-ROOM TEACHER: This boy is near the bottom of his class in achievement. Many teachers have commented to me about his poor work.

ADVISER: Poor worker. Very low in achievement. Interested only in athletics. Talks of being a professional athlete.

B

| YEARLY RECORD FOR GRADE __10__ | | | | Accelerated Science ____ |
| NAME __Burt Ingram__ | | AGE: __16__ | | Regular Class ____ |

Intelligence Test	IQ	Achievement Test	Percentile Rank	Kuder Interest Area	Percentile Rank

HOME-ROOM TEACHER: Inferior ability and achievement. Does failing work in most of his classes.

ADVISER: No interest in school or any of his classes. Spends most of his time with his gang hanging around street corners. Below average in ability and achievement.

A

YEARLY RECORD FOR GRADE 10					Accelerated Science ___ Regular Class ___
NAME Morton Dawson		AGE: 16			
Intelligence Test	IQ	Achievement Test	Percentile Rank	Kuder Interest Area	Percentile Rank
				Mechanical	17
				Computational	28
				Scientific	31
				Persuasive	62
				Artistic	24
				Literary	23
				Musical	19
				Social Service	48
				Clerical	71

HOME-ROOM TEACHER: Poor student. Limited ability.

ADVISER: Plans to become a chemist like his father and brother but his low ability and achievement make this possibility unlikely.

B

YEARLY RECORD FOR GRADE 10					Accelerated Science ___ Regular Class ___
NAME Catherine Kenny		AGE: 16			
Intelligence Test	IQ	Achievement Test	Percentile Rank	Kuder Interest Area	Percentile Rank
		Reading	26	Mechanical	23
		Science	26	Computational	21
		Math	24	Scientific	18
		Social Studies	23	Persuasive	49
				Artistic	53
				Literary	57
				Musical	36
				Social Service	72
				Clerical	89

HOME-ROOM TEACHER: Catherine is a very conscientious student who gets along well with everyone. Although she works very hard and gets good marks she does not always seem to "grasp" the essentials.

ADVISER: Is seriously considering becoming a high-school science teacher.

A

| YEARLY RECORD FOR GRADE __10__ | | | | Accelerated Science ____ | |
| NAME __Paul Kilgore__ | | AGE: __16__ | | Regular Class ____ | |

Intelligence Test	IQ	Achievement Test	Percentile Rank	Kuder Interest Area	Percentile Rank
OTIS:	121	Reading	81	Mechanical	85
		Science	83	Computational	87
		Math	84	Scientific	85
		Social Studies	82	Persuasive	41
				Artistic	16
				Literary	22
				Musical	19
				Social Service	38
				Clerical	21

HOME-ROOM TEACHER: I have heard two different teachers comment on Paul's lackadaisical attitude and class work, and I agree with them. His ability and achievement are both below average and his interest in his studies is nil.

ADVISER: Paul is a difficult boy to talk to. When I try to get at the reason for his poor school work and total lack of interest he clams up and I get no where. His lack of ability is as apparent to all of his teachers as it is to me.

B

| YEARLY RECORD FOR GRADE __10__ | | | | Accelerated Science ____ | |
| NAME __Keith Warren__ | | AGE: __16__ | | Regular Class ____ | |

Intelligence Test	IQ	Achievement Test	Percentile Rank	Kuder Interest Area	Percentile Rank
OTIS:	123	Reading	84	Mechanical	33
		Science	81	Computational	45
		Math	81	Scientific	37
		Social Studies	83	Persuasive	81
				Artistic	69
				Literary	67
				Musical	52
				Social Service	86
				Clerical	49

HOME-ROOM TEACHER: This boy is extremely negative toward his work. He has come into serious conflict with two of his teachers. His achievement is very low, and in ability he is near the bottom of his class.

ADVISER:

A

YEARLY RECORD FOR GRADE __10__ NAME __Bill Turner__ AGE: __16__			Accelerated Science ____ Regular Class ____	
Intelligence Test	IQ	Achievement Test	Percentile Rank	Kuder Interest Area	Percentile Rank
California Test of Mental Maturity:	123	Reading Science Math Social Studies	64 44 41 72	Mechanical Computational Scientific Persuasive Artistic Literary Musical Social Service Clerical	36 50 41 63 81 78 82 46 79

HOME-ROOM TEACHER: Bill's ability is questionable. His teachers tell me that they frequently doubt that the work he hands in is his own. He rarely recites in class or enters into the discussion, and when called on he seems not to understand the question.

ADVISER: Bill's parents have talked with me about whether to send him to college, but I doubt that he has the ability. Various comments about his behavior in class from teachers tend to support my judgment in this.

B

YEARLY RECORD FOR GRADE __10__ NAME __Norman Richardson__ AGE: __16__			Accelerated Science ____ Regular Class ____	
Intelligence Test	IQ	Achievement Test	Percentile Rank	Kuder Interest Area	Percentile Rank
California Test of Mental Maturity:	108	Reading Science Math Social Studies	23 26 26 24	Mechanical Computational Scientific Persuasive Artistic Literary Musical Social Service Clerical	21 24 24 62 37 39 51 78 61

HOME-ROOM TEACHER:

ADVISER:

A

| YEARLY RECORD FOR GRADE __10__ | | | | Accelerated Science ____ |
| NAME __Joyce Durwith__ | | AGE: __16__ | | Regular Class ____ |

Intelligence Test	IQ	Achievement Test	Percentile Rank	Kuder Interest Area	Percentile Rank
California Test of Mental Maturity:	109				

HOME-ROOM TEACHER: A very capable girl. Does well in all of her classes.

ADVISER: Very good student. Have talked with her about going on to college. She plans to study nuclear physics.

B

| YEARLY RECORD FOR GRADE __10__ | | | | Accelerated Science ____ |
| NAME __Alex Crane__ | | AGE: __16__ | | Regular Class ____ |

Intelligence Test	IQ	Achievement Test	Percentile Rank	Kuder Interest Area	Percentile Rank

HOME-ROOM TEACHER: A top-notch student. Several teachers have commented to me about what a pleasure it is to have Alex in their classes. His work is always well done and always in on time. He seems interested in everything.

ADVISER: This boy's only problem is in deciding what most interests him. He enjoys all of his classes and does very good work in all of them. To date he has considered Law, Medicine, Politics, and Teaching!

A

YEARLY RECORD FOR GRADE __10__					Accelerated Science ____ Regular Class ____	
NAME __Kathy Parker__			AGE: __16__			
Intelligence Test	IQ	Achievement Test	Percentile Rank	Kuder Interest Area		Percentile Rank
				Mechanical		81
				Computational		79
				Scientific		84
				Persuasive		31
				Artistic		64
				Literary		79
				Musical		42
				Social Service		37
				Clerical		61

HOME-ROOM TEACHER: An excellent student. Stands high in all of her classes, but is especially interested in English and literature.

ADVISER: Plans to become a writer. Superior in ability and achievement. I have discussed colleges and college courses with her in detail.

B

YEARLY RECORD FOR GRADE __10__					Accelerated Science ____ Regular Class ____	
NAME __Ruth Changer__			AGE: __16__			
Intelligence Test	IQ	Achievement Test	Percentile Rank	Kuder Interest Area		Percentile Rank
		Reading	65	Mechanical		74
		Science	83	Computational		82
		Math	80	Scientific		86
		Social Studies	63	Persuasive		31
				Artistic		16
				Literary		25
				Musical		33
				Social Service		45
				Clerical		59

HOME-ROOM TEACHER: A bright girl but is below average in achievement. More interested in her duties as cheer-leader than in her school work.

ADVISER: A pleasant and popular girl. Does not work up to her full capability. Plans to become a beautician and work in her sister's beauty parlor.

A

YEARLY RECORD FOR GRADE __10__ NAME __Bernice Eager__ AGE: __16__			Accelerated Science ___ Regular Class ___	
Intelligence Test	IQ	Achievement Test	Percentile Rank	Kuder Interest Area
Kuhlmann-Anderson:	122	Reading Science Math Social Studies	84 84 84 81	Mechanical 87 Computational 85 Scientific 93 Persuasive 40 Artistic 27 Literary 36 Musical 31 Social Service 43 Clerical 22

HOME-ROOM TEACHER: Bernice is extremely bright. She loves her work in home economics and dreams of the day when she will have her own home and family. She has no interest in anything except home-planning and home-management.

ADVISER: This girl's strong interest in home economics and her very high ability has led me to suggest that she enter this field professionally. She will have none of it. She has no interest in anything other than becoming a wife and mother.

B

YEARLY RECORD FOR GRADE __10__ NAME __Carroll Scott__ AGE: __16__			Accelerated Science ___ Regular Class ___	
Intelligence Test	IQ	Achievement Test	Percentile Rank	Kuder Interest Area
OTIS:	120	Reading Science Math Social Studies	81 84 83 81	Mechanical 87 Computational 86 Scientific 93 Persuasive 40 Artistic 18 Literary 26 Musical 38 Social Service 54 Clerical 19

HOME-ROOM TEACHER: Below average in achievement. Work is sloppy and never on time. The only teacher who has not commented on this is the physical education teacher. She _always_ gets A's in physical education.

ADVISER: This girl's low achievement will prevent her from being successful in college. She is planning to attend college, and I have several times warned her that unless her achievement improves she will have difficulty in gaining admittance. She plans to become a physical-education teacher.

A

YEARLY RECORD FOR GRADE <u>10</u>				Accelerated Science ____ Regular Class ____	
NAME <u>Frances DeLong</u>			AGE: <u>16</u>		
Intelligence Test	IQ	Achievement Test	Percentile Rank	Kuder Interest Area	Percentile Rank
OTIS:	129	Reading Science Math Social Studies	84 82 81 31		

HOME-ROOM TEACHER: This girl is a problem! Her work is very poor, her ability is definitely below average, and her attitude toward school and her teachers worse than both. Every teacher complains of her poor attitude and lack of interest.

ADVISER: If this girl has any interests I cannot locate them. I have talked with her several times, but with no success. Her lack of ability and achievement are all part of the same picture.

B

YEARLY RECORD FOR GRADE <u>10</u>				Accelerated Science ____ Regular Class ____	
NAME <u>Darrell O'Rourke</u>			AGE: <u>16</u>		
Intelligence Test	IQ	Achievement Test	Percentile Rank	Kuder Interest Area	Percentile Rank
		Reading Science Math Social Studies	28 17 14 26	Mechanical Computational Scientific Persuasive Artistic Literary Musical Social Service Clerical	42 39 43 84 68 42 27 65 79

HOME-ROOM TEACHER: Below average student, quite limited in ability and achievement. Careless about his work. Dislikes school.

ADVISER: Ability and achievement are both limited.

A

YEARLY RECORD FOR GRADE __10__				Accelerated Science ____ Regular Class ____
NAME __Michael Vaughan__		AGE: __16__		

Intelligence Test	IQ	Achievement Test	Percentile Rank	Kuder Interest Area	Percentile Rank
OTIS:	107	Reading	23	Mechanical	21
		Science	24	Computational	18
		Math	26	Scientific	24
		Social Studies	24	Persuasive	36
				Artistic	41
				Literary	32
				Musical	58
				Social Service	85
				Clerical	79

HOME-ROOM TEACHER: A very hard-working student. Gets good grades.

ADVISER: Mike plans to become a high-school science teacher and I have encouraged him in this. I talked with his chemistry teacher who told me of the excellent work Mike did on his science projects. It seems as though he spent more time and did a more thorough job than anyone else in the class.

B

YEARLY RECORD FOR GRADE __10__				Accelerated Science ____ Regular Class ____
NAME __Robert Elliott__		AGE: __16__		

Intelligence Test	IQ	Achievement Test	Percentile Rank	Kuder Interest Area	Percentile Rank
California Test of Mental Maturity:	108	Reading	24		
		Science	26		
		Math	26		
		Social Studies	23		

HOME-ROOM TEACHER: Robert is a capable and hard-working student. He does good work in all of his classes. His ability is well above average.

ADVISER: Plans to become a chemist or a physician. Does excellent work in his science classes.

Thank you for your cooperation. Please put the questionnaire in the accompanying envelope, seal the envelope, write your name on the *outside* of the envelope, and give it to your school principal. Your responses will be kept strictly confidential.

APPENDIX III

TESTING PROGRAM QUESTIONNAIRE

The University of Pittsburgh in conjunction with Russell Sage Foundation of New York has been given support by the U.S. Office of Education to study the consequences of ability testing in schools. Aptitude and achievement tests have sometimes been criticized on the basis of conjecture and not on scientifically established facts. It is our hope through this study to obtain accurate information about this important area.

We would greatly appreciate your cooperation in completing the following questionnaire concerning your school and the school testing program. Your answers will be kept strictly confidential. No school or individual will be identified in our reports.

University of Pittsburgh
Russell Sage Foundation
1964

186

Name of school _____

City _____ State _____

School code number _____ Date _____

Directions: Please place all of your answers in this booklet. Answer each question as accurately as possible but do not spend too much time on any one question. ALL ANSWERS ARE STRICTLY CONFIDENTIAL.

Answer each question as indicated; place an "X" in the parentheses to the left of the answer you choose or write your answer in the space provided. If you choose the option "other (specify)" for any question, be sure to write in your answer on the line provided as well as marking an "X" in the parentheses.

1. Your official position:

( ) 1. Director of Guidance and Counseling
( ) 2. Counselor (not director)
( ) 3. Principal
( ) 4. Assistant Principal
( ) 5. Other (specify) _____
_____

2. Which descriptive phrase below best describes your school?

( ) 1. Comprehensive high school
( ) 2. Academic college preparatory school
( ) 3. Technical high school
( ) 4. Commercial high school
( ) 5. Vocational high school
( ) 6. Other

3. Write in the number of pupils now in grade 12 of your school.

_____ 12th-grade students

4. Write in the number of pupils now in grades 10, 11, and 12 in your school.

_____ students in grades 10, 11, and 12

5. Write in the approximate percentage of pupils in grades 10, 11, and 12 in your school who are in each type of program listed below. (The percentages should add to 100%.)

_____% 1. College preparatory program
_____% 2. Commercial or business program
_____% 3. Vocational, technical, or agricultural program
_____% 4. General program
_____% 5. Other program
100 % TOTAL

6. Grades included in your school:

( ) 1. K–12 or 1–12
( ) 2. 7–12
( ) 3. 8–11
( ) 4. 9–12
( ) 5. 10–12
( ) 6. 11–14
( ) 7. Other (specify) _____
_____

7. Write in the approximate percentage of boys who enter your grade 10 but drop out of school without graduating. (Do not include transfers to other schools.)

_____%

8. Write in the approximate percentage of girls who enter your grade 10 but drop out of school without graduating. (Do not include transfers to other schools.)

_____%

9. Write in the approximate percentage of boys in your graduating class of June, 1963 who have already enrolled in the types of schools listed below.

_____% 1. Four-year college
_____% 2. Junior college
_____% 3. Business school (not in a college or university)
_____% 4. Technical school (not in a college or university)

_____% 5. Some other type of school for high-school graduates

10. Write in the approximate percentage of girls in your graduating class of June, 1963 who have already enrolled in the types of schools listed below.

_____% 1. Four-year college
_____% 2. Junior college
_____% 3. Business school (not in a college or university)
_____% 4. Technical school (not in a college or university)
_____% 5. Some other type of school for high-school graduates

11. Which one of the descriptive phrases below best describes the homes of most of the pupils in your school?

( ) 1. Low-cost single houses
( ) 2. Moderate-priced single houses
( ) 3. Expensive single houses
( ) 4. Low-rental apartments
( ) 5. Moderate-rental apartments
( ) 6. High-rental apartments

12. From which one of the following types of areas do most of the pupils in your school come?

( ) 1. Urban residential
( ) 2. Urban commercial or industrial
( ) 3. Suburban residential
( ) 4. Suburban commercial or industrial
( ) 5. Small towns (under 5,000 population)
( ) 6. Rural or farm

13. Approximately what percentage of the fathers of your pupils in grades 10–12 are in professional, technical, or managerial occupations?

_____%

14. Write in the average number of years of teaching experience of men at the time they begin their first year of teaching in your school.

_____ years

15. Write in the average annual salary of men during their first year of

teaching in your school. (This may not be their first year of teaching in any school.)

$_____

16. Write in the average per-pupil expenditure for all purposes in your school system last year, grades 10–12 only.

$_____ per grade 10–12 pupil

17. Write in the approximate percentage of pupils in grades 10–12 in your school who are:

_____% 1. of Spanish or Latin-American background
_____% 2. of oriental background
_____% 3. American Indians
_____% 4. Negroes

18. Are the following types of marks given regularly in your school?

(1) (2)
Yes No
( ) ( ) 1. Marks that show the level of a pupil's achievement according to standards set by his subject-matter teacher
( ) ( ) 2. Marks that show the level of a pupil's achievement according to standards set by the school system
( ) ( ) 3. Marks that show the level of a pupil's effort according to standards set by his own subject-matter teacher
( ) ( ) 4. Marks that show the level of a pupil's achievement relative to the average achievement in his class group
( ) ( ) 5. Marks that show the level of a pupil's achievement relative to his own level of mental ability
( ) ( ) 6. Marks that show the level of a pupil's achievement relative to his own level of effort

19. Are the following provisions for homogeneous grouping of pupils made in your school?

(1) (2)
Yes No
( ) ( ) 1. Pupils are grouped by mental ability in a few subjects.
( ) ( ) 2. Pupils are grouped by achievement level in a few subjects.
( ) ( ) 3. Pupils are grouped by mental ability in most subjects.
( ) ( ) 4. Pupils are grouped by achievement in most subjects.

buses but cover more subject matter than other classes.
( ) ( ) 3. We do not group them separately but we encourage them to take the Advanced Placement Tests.
( ) ( ) 4. We offer one or more courses that use syllabuses of the Advanced Placement Program.
( ) ( ) 5. We make other provisions not listed above.

20. Mark one or more of the following to show what special provisions, if any, are made for top-ranking pupils in your school.

(1) (2)
Yes No
( ) ( ) 1. We make no special provisions.
( ) ( ) 2. We group them in classes that use our own sylla-

21. Except for the reading test used in this project, are any standardized tests, inventories, or questionnaires given to pupils in your school?

( ) 1. Yes.
( ) 2. No.

If you answered "No" to question 21, omit questions 22–79, and go directly to question 68.

22–34. Please indicate by marking with an "X" the types of standardized tests that have been administered during the past three years to pupils who attend your school and the individuals or groups to whom they are administered.

	Not given	All pupils in grade:			Individuals or groups of pupils in grade:		
		10	11	12	10	11	12
22. Achievement tests	( )	( )	( )	( )	( )	( )	( )
23. Group intelligence tests (Otis, etc.)	( )	( )	( )	( )	( )	( )	( )
24. Individual intelligence tests (Wechsler, etc.)	( )	( )	( )	( )	( )	( )	( )
25. Multi-aptitude tests	( )	( )	( )	( )	( )	( )	( )
26. National college-admissions tests (CEEB, ACT, etc.)	( )	( )	( )	( )	( )	( )	( )
27. National scholarship tests (National Merit, Westinghouse, etc.)	( )	( )	( )	( )	( )	( )	( )
28. Statewide testing programs (Iowa, etc.)	( )	( )	( )	( )	( )	( )	( )
29. Special talents tests (music, art, etc.)	( )	( )	( )	( )	( )	( )	( )
30. Interest inventories	( )	( )	( )	( )	( )	( )	( )
31. Personality inventories	( )	( )	( )	( )	( )	( )	( )
32. Projective tests of personality (TAT, etc.)	( )	( )	( )	( )	( )	( )	( )
33. Biographical data inventories	( )	( )	( )	( )	( )	( )	( )
34. Other (specify) ————————	( )	( )	( )	( )	( )	( )	( )

35. Are standardized achievement tests given in grades 10, 11, and 12 in your school in one or more of the following fields?

(1) (2)
Yes No
( ) ( ) 1. English fundamentals
( ) ( ) 2. Reading comprehension
( ) ( ) 3. Foreign language
( ) ( ) 4. Social studies
( ) ( ) 5. Biological science
( ) ( ) 6. Physical science
( ) ( ) 7. Mathematics
( ) ( ) 8. Other (specify) _____

Please use the following scale in answering questions 36–50.

1. Of no importance
2. Of very little importance
3. Fairly important
4. Very important

For questions 36–50, write in the parentheses the number of the phrase in the scale given above that best indicates the degree of importance attached to each of the following possible reasons for using tests in your school.

36. ( ) To meet state testing requirements

37. ( ) To section pupils in any given course by achievement level

38. ( ) To section pupils in any given grade by level of mental ability

39. ( ) To help in guiding pupils into appropriate curricula (commercial, college-preparatory, vocational, etc.)

40. ( ) To select among applicants for admission to your school

41. ( ) To compare the average scores of pupils with those of other schools

42. ( ) To measure the level of achievement of individual pupils at the end of a school year

43. ( ) To measure the gain in achievement made by individual pupils during a school year

44. ( ) To measure the average gain in achievement made by all pupils in a given course during a school year

45. ( ) To help pupils gain a better understanding of their strengths and weaknesses

46. ( ) To help in educational and vocational counseling of pupils

47. ( ) To help in counseling parents

48. ( ) To evaluate the school curriculum

49. ( ) To evaluate teacher effectiveness

50. ( ) To _____
(Write in any reason not given and rate its importance.)

Please use the following scale in answering questions 51–66.

1. Never
2. Occasionally
3. Frequently
4. Very often

For questions 51–66, write in the parentheses the number of the word or phrase in the scale given above that best indicates how frequently scores from intelligence, scholastic-aptitude, or achievement tests are used in your school for each of the purposes listed below.

51. ( ) To diagnose reasons for failure to learn on the part of pupils

52. ( ) To assess pupil achievement

53. ( ) To provide a basis for school marks

54. ( ) To assess the potential learning ability of pupils

55. ( ) To provide a basis for individualizing instruction

56. ( ) To identify pupils who are under-achievers or over-achievers

57. ( ) To guide pupils in their choices of specific high-school subjects

58. ( ) To guide pupils in their choices of curricula (college-preparatory, commercial, vocational, etc.)

59. ( ) To guide pupils in their decisions about post-high-school education

60. ( ) To guide pupils in their choices of specific colleges

61. ( ) To guide pupils in their choices of occupations

62. ( ) To inform institutions of higher learning about their applicants for admission

63. ( ) To inform prospective employers about job applicants

64. ( ) To inform pupils about their own abilities and achievements

65. ( ) To inform teachers about the abilities and achievements of their pupils

66. ( ) To _____
(Write in any purpose not given and rate its frequency of use.)

67. Write in the average number of hours that pupils spend taking standardized tests given by your school during their twelfth-grade year.

_____ hours

68. Write in the average number of hours that pupils spend taking standardized tests given by outside agencies (CEEB, ACT, National Merit, etc.) during their twelfth-grade year.

_____ hours

69. How does your school report the results of externally sponsored tests (CEEB, ACT, etc.) to pupils and parents?
( ) 1. The results are not reported in school.
( ) 2. Only the scores themselves are reported.
( ) 3. Only an interpretation of the scores is reported.
( ) 4. Both the scores themselves and an interpretation of them are reported.

70. How does your school report the results of tests sponsored by the school?
( ) 1. The results are not reported in school.
( ) 2. Only the scores themselves are reported.
( ) 3. Only an interpretation of the scores is reported.
( ) 4. Both the scores themselves and an interpretation of them are reported.

71. In which one of the following ways has the Parent Teachers Association had the greatest effect on your school's testing program during the last five years?
( ) 1. It has had no effect at all.
( ) 2. It has increased the program.
( ) 3. It has decreased the program.
( ) 4. It has changed the program in some other way.
( ) 5. It has never considered the program.
( ) 6. There is no Parent Teachers Association.

72. To what extent are the parents of pupils in your school provided with information about their children's aptitudes for learning school subjects?

( ) 1. This is never done.

( ) 2. This is done if the parents specially request it.

( ) 3. This is done if a teacher, guidance counselor, or principal takes the initiative in doing it.

( ) 4. This is done routinely on all report cards.

73. Is your school planning to make any significant changes in its testing program between the school years 1963–1964 and 1964–1965?

( ) 1. Yes.

( ) 2. No.

If you answered "No" to question 73, omit questions 74–83, and go directly to question 84.

Please use the following scale for answering questions 74–83.

1. This change is not needed or planned.

2. This change is needed but is not planned.

3. This change is planned but is not needed.

4. This change is both needed and planned.

For questions 74–83 write in the parentheses the number of the statement in the scale above that best indicates your reaction to each change suggested in your school testing program.

74. ( ) To introduce or use more multi-aptitude tests

75. ( ) To introduce or use more standardized achievement tests

76. ( ) To introduce or use more interest inventories

77. ( ) To introduce or use more personality inventories

78. ( ) To improve the scoring of tests

79. ( ) To improve the recording of test scores

80. ( ) To improve the processing and reporting of test results to teachers, counselors, and administrators

81. ( ) To improve the interpretation of test results to pupils and their parents

82. ( ) To improve the interpretation of test results to teachers, counselors, and administrators

83. ( ) To make some other change (Specify) _____

84. Does your school have a guidance program in which at least one person has been officially assigned, part time or full time, to counseling with pupils individuallly?

( ) 1. Yes.

( ) 2. No.

85. Does your school have definite plans to establish a counseling and guidance program within three years?

( ) 1. We already have a guidance program.

( ) 2. No, we have no definite plans to do this.

( ) 3. Yes, in 1964–1965.

( ) 4. Yes, in 1965–1966.

( ) 5. Yes, in 1966–1967.

Thank you for your cooperation.

APPENDIX IV

Familiarity of secondary school teachers with various standardized ability, personality, and interest tests (Percentages)

	NEVER HEARD OF TEST	RECOGNIZE NAME, NO OTHER KNOWLEDGE	KNOW GENERALLY WHAT TEST MEASURES	EXAMINED OR STUDIED ABOUT TEST	NUMBER OF TEACHERS
Stanford-Binet Intelligence Test					
Public	4.5	13.1	41.0	41.3	(1418)
Private	13.2	11.8	47.4	27.6	(152)
Parochial	7.7	14.8	32.4	45.1	(142)
Wechsler Intelligence Scales					
Public	40.7	21.6	22.8	15.0	(1402)
Private	38.5	20.9	29.7	10.8	(148)
Parochial	56.4	17.1	14.3	12.1	(140)
Bell Adjustment Inventory					
Public	60.5	23.1	11.3	5.0	(1394)
Private	80.3	15.0	2.0	2.7	(147)
Parochial	66.7	18.4	11.3	3.5	(141)
Strong Vocational Interest Blanks					
Public	50.8	18.0	16.8	14.5	(1395)
Private	65.8	15.1	11.0	8.2	(146)
Parochial	56.0	19.1	14.9	9.9	(141)

193

Familiarity of secondary school teachers with various standardized ability, personality, and interest tests (Percentages)—continued

	NEVER HEARD OF TEST	RECOG- NIZE NAME, NO OTHER KNOWL- EDGE	KNOW GENER- ALLY WHAT TEST MEAS- URES	EXAM- INED OR STUDIED ABOUT TEST	NUMBER OF TEACHERS
Differential Aptitude Tests					
Public	38.7	26.9	20.7	13.7	(1389)
Private	56.8	18.9	13.5	10.8	(148)
Parochial	44.6	27.3	15.8	12.2	(139)
Minnesota Multiphasic Personality Inventory					
Public	48.1	22.0	15.0	14.8	1389)
Private	74.3	12.8	8.1	4.7	(148)
Parochial	56.7	17.0	14.9	11.3	(141)
Kuder Preference Record, Vocational Form C					
Public	20.7	17.8	26.0	35.5	(1414)
Private	46.7	13.3	20.7	19.3	(150)
Parochial	14.8	9.2	23.2	52.8	(142)
California Test of Mental Maturity					
Public	18.6	22.5	26.2	32.8	(1410)
Private	48.6	23.6	17.6	10.1	(148)
Parochial	14.0	9.8	23.1	53.1	(143)
California Test of Personality					
Public	32.6	26.7	24.1	16.6	(1393)
Private	62.4	21.5	10.1	6.0	(149)
Parochial	25.0	26.4	27.1	21.4	(140)
Otis Quick-Scoring Test of Mental Ability					
Public	20.0	26.2	25.5	28.2	(1413)
Private	15.2	27.2	31.8	25.8	(141)
Parochial	4.9	13.4	20.4	61.3	(142)
Lorge-Thorndike Intelligence Tests					
Public	48.1	27.1	16.0	8.7	(1400)
Private	61.7	20.3	13.4	4.0	(149)
Parochial	51.4	20.7	14.3	13.6	(140)

194

Familiarity of secondary school teachers with various standardized ability, personality, and interest tests (Percentages)—continued

	NEVER HEARD OF TEST	RECOGNIZE NAME, NO OTHER KNOWLEDGE	KNOW GENERALLY WHAT TEST MEASURES	EXAMINED OR STUDIED ABOUT TEST	NUMBER OF TEACHERS
Iowa Tests of Educational Development					
Public	15.2	22.6	24.3	37.9	(1412)
Private	38.5	26.4	20.9	14.2	(148)
Parochial	19.6	23.1	14.0	43.4	(143)
School and College Ability Tests (SCAT)					
Public	25.2	26.8	28.6	19.4	(1407)
Private	28.5	21.2	30.5	19.9	(151)
Parochial	17.7	12.8	28.4	41.1	(141)
Sequential Tests of Educational Progress (STEP)					
Public	59.6	19.8	13.7	6.9	(1398)
Private	63.3	15.0	11.6	10.2	(147)
Parochial	51.8	17.0	14.2	17.0	(141)
College Board Scholastic Aptitude Test (SAT)					
Public	10.0	24.1	38.6	27.3	(1414)
Private	.7	4.6	38.6	56.2	(153)
Parochial	3.5	12.0	35.9	48.6	(142)
Preliminary Scholastic Aptitude Test (PSAT)					
Public	26.2	24.2	31.3	18.3	(1406)
Private	9.2	8.6	36.2	46.1	(152)
Parochial	7.7	9.9	28.9	53.5	(142)

Index

Index

ACCURACY of tests
  teachers' opinions about, 50–54
  in relation to background char-
    acteristics, 54
Achievement vs. ascription, 2–3
Achievement tests
  coaching for, 107–125
  extent of use
    in elementary schools, 17–18
    in secondary schools, 13–16
Advising students about course work
  vs. card sort test score, 101
  vs. experience in administering of
    scoring tests, 84
  vs. familiarity with tests, 84
  use of test scores for, by teachers,
    82–86, 133–134
American Council on Education, 129
American Institute for Research,
    xix, 7
American Psychological Association,
    129
Anastasi, Anne, 17
Armitage, Peter, 47
Ascription vs. achievement, 2–3

BOONE, Barbara, xix
Brennan, William, 136
Brim, Orville G., Jr., xix, 5, 7, 32,
    66, 136, 143, 151
Buck, Vernon, 5

CARD sort test, 98–106
  vs. index of extent of testing, 106
  vs. index of extent of test use,
    105–106
  vs. opinion about accuracy of
    tests, 103
  vs. school and testing program
    characteristics, 105–106
  vs. teacher opinions and back-
    ground characteristics, 102

vs. teacher reports of test score use,
    100–102
  vs. use of test scores in advising
    pupils about course work, 101
Carnegie Corporation of New York,
    xix
Coaching for tests, 107–125, 137–138
  effect on curriculum, 137–138
  reports of teachers on, 111–119
  student reports on, 119–121
  teacher opinions on, 109–111
Cochran, W. G., 47
College Board, 41–42
College Entrance Examination Board,
    107–108, 120
Cooley, William W., xix
Cooperative Research Branch, United
    States Office of Education, xix

DAILEY, John T., xix, 12, 143, 144
D'Amour, O'Neil C., 148
Data
  analysis, 150–151
  collection procedures, 149–150
  sources of, 7–9
Dunne, Margaret, xix

EDUCATIONAL Testing Service, 41–42
Elementary School Testing Survey, 9
Epstein, Roberta R., xix, 9, 13, 18, 88
Experience of teachers with tests and
    testing, 33–48
  vs. reporting of general information
    about intelligence to pupils, 93
  vs. use of intelligence test scores in
    advising pupils about course
    work, 84
Extent of testing
  in elementary schools, 17–18
  in secondary schools, 13–16
  opinions of teachers about, 61–63

FAMILIARITY of teachers with tests, 38–42, 193–195
vs. number of courses in tests and measurement, 47
vs. reporting of general information about intelligence to pupils, 93
vs. use of test scores in advising pupils about course work, 84
Firestone, Ira, xix
Flanagan, John C., xix, *12, 13, 143, 145*

GENETIC vs. learning components in tested intelligence
opinions of teachers about, 59–60, 131–132
vs. background characteristics, 60
Glaser, William A., *95*
Glass, David C., xix, *5, 7, 32, 66, 83, 143*
Goldberg, Isidore, xix, *7, 12, 32, 66, 143*
Goslin, David A., *1, 3, 7, 9, 12, 13, 18, 32, 59, 66, 83, 88, 102, 143*
Grading pupils
use of test scores in, by teachers, 80–82, 133–134

HALLOCK, Barbara A., xix, *9, 13, 18, 88*
Hastings, J. Thomas, 99, 100

IMPORTANCE of tested intelligence for success in school and after school
students' opinions about, 55
teachers' opinions about, 54–58
Intelligence tests
elimination of, 132
extent of use of
in elementary schools, 17–18
in secondary schools, 13–16
reporting of results of, by teachers, 89–96, 132–137

JACOBSON, Lenore, *128*

KNOWLEDGE of content of standardized tests, by teachers, 38–42, 193–195
vs. teacher reports of having changed course content, 114–115
vs. teacher reports of having changed teaching methods, 115–117

vs. teacher reports of having coached pupils, 114–117
Kuhn, Eleanor, xix

LAVIN, David E., *4, 67*
Lazarsfeld, Paul F., *95*
Lennon, Roger, xix
Linton, Ralph, 2

MACIVER, Robert M., *95*
Maxwell, Albert E., 47
Merton, Robert K., xix, *95*

NATIONAL Catholic Education Association, 148
National Defense Education Act, 36
National Education Association, 129
Neulinger, John, 5
New York State Regents' Examinations, 107

OBJECTIVE tests vs. essay tests, teacher reports of the use of, 122–125, 137
Opinions of teachers, 49–78, 129–133
on accuracy of tests, 50–59, 129–133
vs. use of the test scores in advising pupils about course work, 85
vs. card sort test scores, 102–105
on coaching for tests, 109–111, 137–138
on genetic vs. learning components in tested intelligence, 59–60, 129–133
vs. use of test scores in advising pupils about course work, 85
on number of tests being given, 61–63
vs. practices, 92–95, 138–139
on providing pupils and parents with intelligence test scores, 72–78, 133–137
vs. students' opinions, 77–78
on relevance of tested intelligence to success in school and after school, 54–58, 130
on testing practices, 60–78
on the use of test scores in assigning grades, 71–72
on the use of tests to evaluate teachers, 70–71
vs. school policy, 72
on weight to be given test scores, 63–70, 130
Orr, David G., *12, 143*

PROJECT talent, xix, 7, 12, 13, 32,
    87, 144

REPORTING of test scores to pupils
    and parents
    vs. familiarity and experience with
        tests, 93
    vs. opinion about giving informa-
        tion to pupils, 94
    opinions of pupils about, 77
    opinions of teachers about, 72–78,
        132–137
    school policies on, 25–32
    by teachers, 87–96
Reporting of test scores to teachers
    opinions of teachers about, 76
    school policies on, 32
    teacher reports of, 88–89
Rosenthal, Robert, 128, 131
Russell Sage Foundation program of
    research on the social conse-
    quences of testing, 4–5, 7, 9, 144,
    150, 153, 186

SAMPLE selection, 143–149
Sarason, Seymour B., 46
Self-fulfilling prophecies, tests as,
    128–129
Shaycoft, Marion F., 12, 143, 145
Social consequences of testing, 4–5,
    7, 9, 144, 150, 153, 186
Social differentiation, 1
Standardized tests
    extent of use of, 3–4, 13–19
    opinions of teachers about accuracy
        of, 50–54
    reasons for development of, 3
    teachers' uses of, 79–106
    uses of, in schools and colleges, 4,
        12–32

TEACHERS
    access to test scores, 88–89
    experience in administering tests,
        42–46
    experience with tests and testing,
        33–48
        vs. background characteristics,
            46–48
    familiarity with tests, 38–42,
        193–195
    formal training in measurement
        techniques, 34–38, 127–129
    opinions of, regarding tests, 49–78,
        129–133
    opinions of, on coaching for tests,
        109–111

    role in counseling and advising
        students, 134
    role in testing and evaluation, 5–6,
        139–140
    uses of tests, 79–106, 133–137
Teachers' card sort, 169–185
Teachers' questionnaire, 153–185
Testing
    extent of, in schools, 13–18
    in the Soviet Union, 3
    opinions of teachers about, 60–78
    Russell Sage Foundation research
        program on the social con-
        sequences of, 4–5, 7, 9, 150,
        153, 186
Testing Program Questionnaire, 186–
    192
Test scores
    practices of teachers regarding,
        87–96
    reporting of, to pupils and parents,
        school policies on, 25–32,
        135–137
    opinions of teachers about, 72–
        78, 132–133
    reporting of, to teachers, 32, 76,
        88–89
    uses of, by teachers, 79–106
Training of teachers in measurement
    techniques, 34–38, 127–129
    vs. background characteristics,
        35–38

UDY, Stanley H., Jr., 5
United States Office of Education,
    xix, 148, 153, 186
University of Pittsburgh, xix, 144,
    148, 150, 153, 186
Uses of standardized test results,
    19–25
    in elementary schools, 23–25
    in secondary schools, 19–23
    vs. opinions, 92–95, 138–139
    opinions of teachers about, 63–78
    by teachers, 79–106
        in advising pupils about their
            work, 82–86
        in grading pupils, 80–82
        in providing pupils and their
            parents with information
            about their abilities, 87–96,
            132–137

WASHINGTON, Robert, xix
Weight indices, 63–66, 112

YATES, Frank, 47

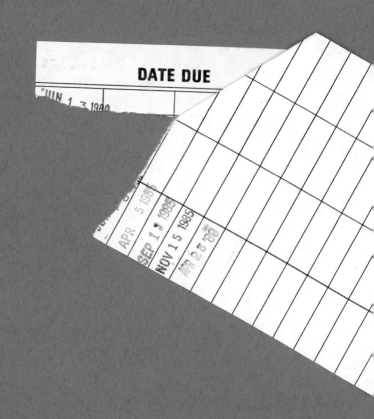